Pattaya

Youtuber

And other true stories from Thailand

By Walt Gleeson

Note from author

This collection includes some of the stories I have heard about Thailand over the years. All the stories are based on true events, but I have changed the names of the people and some other minor details to protect the privacy of all involved.

Also by this author

Lost in Yaba: Down and Out in Laos

Quiet in the Corner

Table of Contents

Honeymoon Nightmare

When my wife (Hannah) and I were discussing where to go on our honeymoon, we initially decided on a week of luxury in the Maldives, but after we looked into the cost of it, we thought it would make more sense to use that money to go backpacking for a month instead. Hannah had never been to Southeast Asia before, but she knew that I had been several times and that I loved it. We decided to fly into Bangkok and spend four weeks travelling around three or four countries, with Bali as our final destination. We agreed to travel on a low budget for the four weeks, but we wanted to stay somewhere more up-market at our first and last destinations. It was my job to book nice hotels in Bangkok and Bali. I had been to Bangkok many times before - the last time was five years ago - but I had always stayed in cheap guesthouses around

Kao San Road. I didn't know any nice hotels in Bangkok. I had been to the Sukhumvit area on a few nights out, but I didn't want to spend my honeymoon anywhere near there because of Nana Plaza and all the freelancers standing by the side of the road. I told Hannah I was having difficulty choosing which area of Bangkok to stay in.

"Okay, Chris, I'll look into it," she said. "I'll read up on Bangkok, and I'll tell you the area I want to stay in. Then you can choose a hotel in that area."

A few days later, she came back to me.

"From what I saw online, the area around Terminal 21 will be fine," she said.

"Terminal 21?" I had never heard of it.

"It's a shopping mall. It looks cool, and people say there are a lot of shops and restaurants nearby. There's also a Skytrain station there."

"Okay. I'll look into it."

I was disappointed to see that Terminal 21 was in Sukhumvit. I really didn't want to stay there. But as I continued to search for hotels in Bangkok, I realized that Sukhumvit was huge, and a lot of the hotels I liked were in that area. I spent a few days comparing all the hotels around Terminal 21, and I ended up choosing a place called 'Jasmine City Hotel.' I chose it because the rooms were really big, it had a beautiful rooftop swimming pool, and the reviews were generally very good. From what I could make out on Google maps, it also looked to be very conveniently located.

It was within walking distance of Terminal 21 and Asok BTS (Skytrain) station, and although it was in Sukhumvit, it looked like it was miles away from Nana Plaza.

We landed in Suvarnabhumi Airport on the stroke of midnight. We had a taxi booked. My days of cheap tourist buses to Kao San Road were behind me. Hannah fell asleep as soon as we pulled onto the highway. I wanted to stay awake and catch my first glimpse of Thailand in five years. It felt very strange to be back in the land of smiles as a married man. I had been to Thailand three times before, each time on my own. I spent most of my time enjoying the nightlife in Bangkok, Pattaya, Phuket and some other islands down south. Now I was travelling with my wife and I was excited about experiencing Thailand in a completely different way. Hannah had plans to do a lot of shopping, visit temples, do a Thai cooking course and try various water sports. I had never bothered with any of that stuff during my previous trips.

It was almost two AM by the time we got off the highway and entered the city. The streets were very quiet. Almost everywhere was closed, and we didn't pass any famous landmarks so I didn't have a clue where we were. Then I saw two white men walking along the street, so I figured we must be in Sukhumvit - the main tourist area of Bangkok. I heard loud music up ahead. Hannah woke up and looked out the window with me. None of the stores or restaurants were open on the main street. Everywhere looked grey in the darkness, but among the dullness there was one small side street that was full of light. This side street was lined with bars and huge neon lights. There were falangs and Thai women flowing in and out. *What is this place?* I asked myself, and then I looked up and saw a sign that read, 'Soi Cowboy'. I had read about Soi Cowboy a lot online, and I had one vague memory of making the long walk from Nana Plaza to Soi Cowboy one night long ago when I was very drunk. It was good to see this famous street again. Our taxi turned left, went straight for a hundred meters and then turned off the main street onto a narrow side street. *Oh no!* I thought. *Our hotel cannot be here.* We passed several alcohol carts and small bars full of Thai women.

"What kind of bars are they?" Hannah asked.

"Don't know," I mumbled, embarrassed that my wife had to see this kind of place.

About seventy meters up ahead I could see the bottom of Soi Cowboy. *Please keep driving*, I said to myself, but a sign came into view to my right - 'Jasmine City Hotel'. I couldn't believe it. I had accidentally booked a hotel right next to Soi Cowboy. My wife and I would have to spend the first few nights of our honeymoon next to an infamous redlight district. As we were getting out of the taxi, I said to my wife, "I'm sorry. I fucked up. This hotel is right next to a really famous nightlife area, but I had no idea when I booked it."

"It's okay," she said, looking very tired and irritable. "Let's just check in."

We checked in quickly and headed up to our room on the

fifteenth floor. It was a suite, so there was a large living room with a sofa and a dining table. Off to the side there was a small kitchen. Both the bedroom and the bathroom were surprisingly large. Hannah liked the room at first, but when she tried to wash her hands in the bathroom, she was disgusted to see brown water gush out of the tap. She took it as a sign that the hotel was dirty. But I had come across this brown water a few times in Thailand.

"It's okay. It just means the tap hasn't been used in a while," I said. "Let the water run for a minute and it will be fine."

I apologized to Hannah again for booking into a hotel in a nightlife area.

"It's fine," she said. "We were lucky to get a room so high up. It's really quiet up here."

Hannah still didn't seem to realize that we were staying right next to a redlight district. I wanted her to hear it from me rather than being shocked by it the next day.

"But, you know, Bangkok has three famous redlight districts," I explained awkwardly, "and that busy street we passed is one of them. It's called Soi Cowboy. Most foreigners who come to Bangkok have heard of it."

Hannah didn't say anything. She was busy looking through her luggage for her phone charger.

"But we can stay away from that area at night," I concluded.

We both slept well after our long journey. We were still very tired when we woke up at nine AM but we couldn't get back to sleep. Both of us were feeling lazy so we decided to take it easy until the afternoon. We went downstairs and had a look around the building that was connected to the hotel. There was a Boots, a Subway, several restaurants and a Starbucks. Perfect! We got a coffee and a scone and then went back to our room to laze the morning away.

In the afternoon we decided to go see the Grand Palace. We stood at the side of Sukhumvit Road and hailed down several taxis, but they all refused to put on the meter because the Grand Palace was 'too far' or 'traffic very bad'. It made no sense to me. Even taking into account the bad traffic in the afternoon, I didn't think we should have to pay more than two hundred baht, but they were all quoting us four or five hundred. Crazy! I heard that a taxi to the airport is only three hundred and fifty baht, and that's way outside the city. I couldn't keep my wife waiting at the side of the road under the afternoon sun for long, so when a taxi driver quoted us three hundred baht, I begrudgingly accepted.

I had visited the Grand Palace twice before, but of course it was Hannah's first time. The sun was particularly strong that day so we skipped through the palace grounds without looking at any of the artwork in detail or taking many pictures. Next, we walked to Kao San Road. Hannah had heard a lot about famous Kao San, though she was disappointed when she finally saw it for herself.

"Is this it?" she asked, as we walked past convenience stores, cafes, restaurants, guesthouses, and vendors selling T-shirts and Thai souvenirs.

"It's much more fun at night," I said.

Kao San Road always looks depressing during the day, and in the five years since I had been there, it had hardly changed. There were some new up-market bars and restaurants here and there, but overall the budget backpacking vibe was still strong.

We sat in a restaurant filled with Western backpackers and we enjoyed chicken green curry and Pad Thai for lunch. Many people don't know this, but you can walk from Kao San Road to the river in five minutes. I brought Hannah to a park near the river, and we sat in the shade of some trees, drinking iced coffee. We both agreed that the first day of our honeymoon was a success. We had a lazy morning and a productive afternoon, and now it was time to head back to our hotel. We got lucky with the first taxi we hailed down, as the driver only charged us two hundred baht. He left us off on Sukhumvit Road, and then we walked down the small side street towards our hotel. There was a 7eleven right across from our hotel so we decided to go in to buy some snacks and a few beers. It was great to be in a Thai 7eleven again. They always have a great selection of chocolate, crisps, ramen, energy drinks and loads more. We got a bit over excited by all the delicious-looking food and low prices; we ended up buying a bag full of snacks and a load of beer.

As we stood by the side of the road outside 7eleven, waiting for a gap in the traffic so that we could cross the road to our hotel, I saw a Thai woman dressed all in black walking towards us. I thought nothing of it and just took a quick glance to check her out. I froze when I saw a familiar face looking back at me. It was a woman named Lot who I had been with in Pattaya five years ago. Lot and I made eye contact for only a fraction of a second before I turned away quickly. I desperately hoped that she wouldn't recognize me. Without looking at the traffic, I stepped out onto the road in a panic. A taxi had to slam on the breaks to avoid hitting me. The driver beeped his horn angrily at me. I didn't care. All I cared about was crossing the road before Lot had a chance to remember me and call out my name. Hannah reluctantly followed me as I hurried across the road.

"Chris, what are you doing? You're gonna get us killed," she yelled after me.

I didn't respond. I was terrified that Lot would follow us or shout out something to get my attention.

When we got into the hotel lobby, I felt a bit better. While we were waiting for the elevator, I kept looking over at the hotel entrance to make sure Lot wasn't chasing after me. The elevator was taking a long time.

"Chris, what has gotten into you?" Hannah asked.

"What do you mean?" I was trying to appear calm.

When we finally got into the elevator, we swiped our card to give us access to the fifteenth floor. I felt at ease now that I knew Lot wouldn't be able to follow us.

"Why did you jump in front of that car?" Hannah wouldn't let it drop. "It looked like you were running away from something."

"Don't exaggerate," I said. "That's the way they do it here in Bangkok. The cars don't stop for you unless you walk in front of them."

"Do you realize how crazy that sounds?"

"Yes, but that's just the way it is. You'll be doing it too in a few days."

Back in our room, Hannah went in for a quick show while I had a beer on the sofa. I needed a drink to calm myself down. Now that I had a few minutes to myself, I thought back on my time with Lot. We met five years ago in a bar on Walking Street, Pattaya. We had a few drinks together and I barfined her. We got on so well that I barfined her for the next six days and brought her down to Phuket and Krabi with me. I was twenty-eight at the time. Lot was only twenty-one. I initially barfined Lot because she was beautiful, but I brought her travelling down south with me because she was a lot of fun to be around. She had a very fun-loving personality and she had great banter. When it came time for me to go home, I gave her six thousand baht (a thousand baht for each day she was with me) like we had agreed. We also exchanged emails and promised to stay in touch. We ended up emailing each other every day. I even sent her some pictures of us in bed together. The photos were not sexual in any way; they just showed us lying close together, with the duvet pulled up to our necks. I missed Lot and I wanted to return to Thailand to see her again. But after only a few weeks of emailing each other, she started asking me to send her money. I told her that if I send her money, it would take me much longer to save enough money to return to Thailand to see her. She didn't care about that. Her next email was much longer and more dramatic than usual. She wrote (or someone else wrote for her) a long paragraph about how her mom had recently been hospitalized and how her family were too poor to pay for her treatment. Lot pleaded for my help. I had read about this kind of scam dozens of times online. I saw through her lies straight away. I sent back a brief email saying that I couldn't send her any money, but I hoped her mom got well soon. We emailed each other a few times after that, but within a few weeks we lost touch.

Hannah came out of the shower and started blow drying her hair in front of the mirror in the corner of the room. I got a second beer from the fridge. A thought occurred to me. I reached for my phone and opened up my email. My heart almost jumped out of my throat when I saw that there was an email from Lot in my inbox - the first email from her in almost five years. I looked up at Hannah to make sure she was busy. I kept one eye on her as I opened the email. It was a short email, but it floored me. It read, 'Chris, I see you. Why you run away? You have new girlfriend?'

I closed and opened the email dozens of times over the next half hour, re-reading those three sentences over and over again to make sure I hadn't missed anything. I was in a bad spot. I figured Lot probably worked in a bar on Soi Cowboy, so there was a good chance we would bump into her again over the next few days. I imagined how horribly awkward it would be if she ran up to me on the street and gave me a big hug in front of my wife. I didn't want the last girl I fucked before Hannah to be anywhere near our honeymoon. And I certainly didn't want Hannah finding out that I had been with a prostitute. What a nightmare! I considered emailing Lot back and explaining that I wanted her to pretend not to know me if she saw me again, but I decided against it. I didn't know how Lot felt about me. Perhaps she was still angry that I hadn't sent money to help her mom. If I asked her to pretend not to know me, perhaps she would go out of her way to make trouble for me out of spite. I thought it best to just leave the email unanswered and hope that I would not run into her again.

At 8 PM, Hannah and I were ready to go out for a look around and grab a late dinner. I decided to wear a baseball cap. I never wore baseball caps, but my wife bought one especially for our travels because she was worried that my expanding bald spot would get burned in the Southeast Asian sun. I told her it was a waste of money and a waste of space in our luggage because I would never wear it, so you can imagine how surprised she was when she saw me waiting for her at the door with the cap on.

"What's with the cap?" she asked.

"Just thought I'd give it a try," I said.

"But it's dark outside. You should have worn it today when we went to the temple."

"I know, but I didn't think of it then. I'll wear it every day from now on."

While we were waiting for the elevator, I pulled the cap down low, almost to my eyes. As we were walking out of the hotel, we agreed to head to Terminal 21 to look around for an hour and then go get some Thai food and have a few beers in a quiet bar. We crossed the road towards our local 7eleven. The small bar next to the 7eleven was empty, but there were six Thai women standing in the entrance waiting for customers. I made the mistake of looking up at them. One of them was staring right at me. It was Lot. She waved at me and smiled brightly. Then she held up her phone and made a typing action with her free hand. I guess that was her way of telling me to reply to her email. I frowned at her and shook my head once. I looked over at Hannah. Thankfully she was looking straight ahead and hadn't noticed my brief and silent interaction with Lot. I couldn't believe my horrible luck. Lot was working in a bar right across from where we were staying. We would have to pass her bar every time we went in and out of the hotel. I was now completely reliant on Lot's discretion. But the problem was that Lot was a very impulsive person, and after a few drinks she was very unpredictable and sometimes wild. If Hannah and I passed Lot's bar when she was drunk, God knows what would happen. I needed to talk with Lot quickly.

Terminal 21 was an interesting shopping mall because each floor had a theme of a different country. One of the floors was decked out to look like Japan, another looked like America, and so on. But apart from the cool design, the shopping mall was of no interest to me because it was full of expensive Western brands that I could just as easily buy at home at similar prices. Hannah, on the other hand, enjoyed browsing these familiar brands and comparing the prices and product lines to stores back home. I told Hannah that I wanted to look around the bookshop downstairs, so we agreed to look around separately and rendezvous in front of the information desk in twenty minutes. Hannah went upstairs, and instead of going down to the bookshop, I hurried to the exit and ran back to Lot's bar. She was still standing in the entrance with the other girls. Out of breath, I greeted Lot warmly as an act of diplomacy.

"When you come to Bangkok?" Lot asked me, as she rubbed my right arm affectionately.

She seemed very happy that I had made the effort to come back and talk with her.

"I came late last night."

"For how long?"

"Two more nights. Lot, I thought you live in Pattaya."

"I get bored of Pattaya long time ago, so I move to Phuket for one year, and last year I come to Bangkok. I move, move, move everywhere, no problem."

The last five years had been tough on Lot. She was now under weight and her face was covered in pimples. She never used to wear much makeup, but now she put it on an inch thick to cover her bad skin. Her style had also changed. When I was with her, she looked young and beautiful in cute summer dresses with flower patterns. Now she looked much older in ripped black jeans and a black T-shirt. She looked every bit a hardcore bar girl.

"I see you with girl," Lot said. "She your girlfriend?"

"Yeah, kind of," I replied. "Look, you will probably see us again later, and probably tomorrow too, but can you please pretend not to know me? Is that okay?"

"Chris, I know, I know," Lot laughed. "You with new girlfriend now. You good man to me before. I no make problem for you."

Lot's response was a great relief to me. I wanted to chat with her for a few minutes more to make sure everything was good between us and that we were on the same wavelength, but I was pushed for time. I thanked Lot for understanding my situation and then I ran back to Terminal 21 to meet Hannah. As I was running, I couldn't help but wonder how many men Lot had been with since I had last seen her. Thousands, I reckoned.

After Terminal 21, Hannah and I walked leisurely along Sukhumvit Road. Hannah was glad to find counterfeit handbags, purses and clothing being sold in small street stores and stalls, but she was surprised by the high prices. Even after she haggled with the vendors hard, she never got to a price she was happy with. As we walked along Sukhumvit Road, we saw a lot of ladyboys standing at the side of the road on their own. They stayed perfectly still when we walked by, but we saw them reach out a hand and say things like, 'Handsome man', 'I go with you', or 'I take care you,' to men who were walking alone.

"Are they ladyboys?" Hannah asked.

"Yep."

"What are they doing?"

"I guess they are looking for customers."

This stunned Hannah into silence.

I didn't know the Sukhumvit area well, but I knew that if we kept walking down Sukhumvit Road we would get very close to Nana Plaza. I did not want Hannah to see the Nana area. Soi Cowboy was fifty meters passed the entrance of our hotel, but Hannah didn't walk down that way so she didn't see the Go-go bars. There were ladyboy freelancers along our end of Sukhumvit Road, but there were also a lot of Western couples and families with young children. Hannah viewed it as a tourist area that happened to have a few dodgy bars and freelancers here and there. I knew that if she saw Nana Plaza, her opinion of Sukhumvit would completely change. I had mentioned to her that I had a few nights out in Sukhumvit on my previous trips, so I was worried that if she saw the thousands of prostitutes and sex tourists in and around Nana, she might look at me differently.

Fortunately, it is a long walk from Terminal 21 to Nana Plaza. Hannah got tired after walking a couple of hundred meters and suggested that we have dinner in the next half-decent restaurant we saw. I have no idea about the names of all the sois (streets) off of Sukhumvit Road, but we ended up walking down a soi that had a very Middle Eastern feel to it; a lot of the people were from the Middle East and a lot of the restaurants were selling food from that part of the world. We found a nice Thai restaurant on this soi, and we stuck to Thai food and a few beers to wash it down. After dinner, we walked back in the direction of our hotel and stopped off for a few drinks in a large sports bar along the way. We sat at a table that overlooked the bustling Sukhumvit Road, which meant we could people watch while drinking our beer, but it also meant that street hawkers selling knock-off sunglasses and wooden frogs could easily approach us and pester us to buy their goods.

"It's eleven o' clock at night and the streets are still crowded," Hannah observed.

"This area is famous for its nightlife," I said.

"Where did you drink when you came here?"

"I can't remember, to be honest," I answered, perhaps blushing a little. "Just some random bars."

Hannah started to comment on how there was an unnatural ratio of Thai women to Thai men, and foreign men to foreign women. When Hannah saw a fat old man in his seventies walking down the road with a beautiful Thai girl in her early twenties, she looked at me and asked, "These women only go with men for the money, right?"

"I guess so."

"I think that's disgusting," Hannah said, shaking her head.

I thought how horrified she would be if she knew even half of what I got up to on my previous trips to Thailand.

By the time we got onto our second beer, we moved the conversation onto our plans for the rest of our trip. We both really enjoyed talking about all the beautiful beaches, fun activities and delicious food that awaited us over the coming weeks. This was a trip of a lifetime for us, and the fun was in the planning as much as the doing. At around midnight, we agreed to call it a night. We were both still jetlagged and in desperate need of a good night sleep. After talking with my wife about our exciting plans for the rest of our honeymoon, I was on a high, but as soon as we left the bar, anxiety set in as I started to worry about passing Lot's bar on the way back to our hotel. I knew that one word from Lot could destroy the rest of our honeymoon. I desperately hoped that she would not be drunk. I got lucky. Lot wasn't even in the bar when we passed. She must have gone with a customer. Hannah and I only had one more night in Bangkok; one more night to get through, and then this nightmare would be over.

The next day Hannah and I woke up early and went to

Siam Square on the BTS. On the way I checked my email and I was horrified to see that I had another email from Lot. It read. 'Chris, I have big problem. I need 10,000 baht. Please help.'

I closed my email quickly and put my phone away. I didn't know what to do. Lot had me by the balls. If I refused to give her the money, or even if I chose not to reply to her email, she might get angry at me and make a scene the next time we pass her bar. I regretted coming back to Thailand. We should have splashed out and gone to the Maldives for a week of luxury. Who needs this hassle on their honeymoon! I decided to put the problem with Lot on the long finger. I wanted to spend a lovely morning with my wife, and then after lunch I could think about how to handle Lot.

First Hannah and I looked around some up-market stores in Siam Square and then we moved on to the much cheaper MBK. At noon we walked over to Siam Paragon and spent an hour in Bangkok Ocean World. Hannah had a great time walking around three different shopping malls and an aquarium. I was glad to see her having fun, but my head was miles away and I couldn't enjoy myself. My thoughts kept coming back to Lot and the money. I resolutely came to the conclusion that I would not give Lot anything. If Hannah found out about my relationship with Lot, it might ruin our honeymoon, but if she found out that I gave Lot ten thousand baht during our honeymoon, it might ruin our marriage. And I decided not to reply to Lot's email, in the hope that no definite answer would lead to no definite action.

On the way back to our hotel on the BTS, I checked my email again. There was another email from Lot, only this time she didn't write anything. I was confused. I couldn't understand why she would send me an empty email, but then I noticed two files attached. I angled my phone away from Hannah to make sure she could not see my screen. I wasn't even surprised when I opened the attachments and saw that there were two photos of me and Lot in bed together. I took it as a threat; she would show these pictures to Hannah the next time we passed the bar if I didn't give her the money. Things were getting out of hand. I needed to think up of a plan quickly. Hannah and I only had one night left in Bangkok. I decided I would feign illness so that we wouldn't have to go out at night. We could order room service and have a romantic night in. It was such a simple plan, but it would completely remove any chance of seeing Lot again.

Now that I didn't have to worry about Lot anymore, I wanted to focus on enjoying my time with my wonderful wife. When we got back to the hotel, I suggested we go up to the rooftop pool for a swim. Hannah loved this idea. There was nothing else in particular that we wanted to do in Bangkok, so we agreed that relaxing by the hotel pool would be a great way to spend an evening. Before we left our room, I made sure to rub my forehead slowly a few times so that Hannah would notice.

"Are you okay?" she asked lovingly.

"Yes, I'm fine," I said, with feigned courage. "Just have a bit of a headache, but I'll be fine."

I was just laying the ground for later, when I would have to pretend to be too sick to go out.

The swimming pool was as beautiful as in the pictures. There was a wooden pagoda at the top of the pool, and at the other end there was a fish statue that spurted out a constant stream of water. The sides of the pool were lined with large palm trees. It was a stunning setting, yet we were the only ones there to appreciate it.

"Where is everyone?" Hannah asked. "Why are we the only ones here?"

"Because it's kind of late and it's cloudy."

We walked to the far side of the pool and placed our towels on the two sun beds directly behind the stone fish. Then we pushed the sun beds a little closer and lay down together in complete silence, holding hands. It was perfect. It finally felt like we were on our honeymoon. We stayed like that for almost half an hour. Then we were disturbed by the sound of flip flops dragging along the floor. I opened my eyes and saw a woman in a bikini and baseball cap sit down on a sun bed at the other end of the pool, near the pagoda. It was Lot. I suspected it was her as soon as I saw her, but when she took off the baseball cap there was no mistaking her. *What the fuck are you doing here?* I thought. The cheapest room in the hotel was about three thousand baht a night. I got goose bumps at the thought of her paying all that money just to be near me. *What is she planning?* I kept asking myself.

Now was the time to feign illness and go back to our room for the rest of the day, but before I could say anything, Hannah stood up and stepped towards the edge of the swimming pool.

"Hannah," I called out, but it was too late. She dived into the pool.

When she resurfaced, she wiped the water from her eyes and said, "The water is lovely. Come in for a swim."

"No, no. I'm okay," I replied. "To be honest, my headache is getting worse. Can we go back to our room?"

"You go ahead," she said, with less concern than I had hoped for. "Take an aspirin, lay down on the bed, and I'll be down in twenty minutes."

"No, I'll wait," I said.

There was no way I was going to leave her alone with Lot.

While Hannah was facing me, I could see Lot in the background waving her hand in the air to grab my attention. When I looked up, she pointed to her phone. I took that to mean, 'Check your email'. Sure enough, there was a new email from Lot. It read, 'Well, you help me or no?'

I didn't reply. I was panicking inside. Lot stood up and walked to the edge of the pool. She sat at the edge and let her legs dangle in the cool water. Hannah started swimming towards Lot's end of the pool. My wife loved meeting new people, so she greeted Lot and they ended up chatting. They were out of ear shot from me, but I could see that they were both smiling and getting along well. Then they both looked over at me. Lot waved and shouted out, "Hi, Chris"

I raised my hand awkwardly to return the greeting. I even managed a smile.

"This is Lot," Hannah shouted, looking very happy. "She is telling me about nice places to eat around here."

Hannah turned back to Lot and they started chatting again. I watched them closely, fearing the mood would change and Hannah's facial expressions would darken, but that didn't happen. They were really hitting it off. After ten minutes with Lot, Hannah swam to my end of the pool and asked, "How's your headache?"

"Not good."

"I'm going to swim five more laps and then go. Do you want to go back to the room first, or do you want to wait for me?"

"If you are sure it will only be five more laps, I'll wait."

Hannah started swimming again. Lot was still sitting at the edge of the pool. I got a new email from her that simply read, 'Well?'

This time I replied to her email. I asked 'Why are you in this hotel?'

'My Australian friend stay this hotel three months. I visit him sometime,' she answered. 'You help me or no? I need answer.' 'Okay. I will help you,' I wrote. I had no other choice. 'I will bring the money to your bar tonight. Please don't make any problem.'

Lot seemed happy with my email. She smiled and put her phone down.

After five laps, Hannah pulled herself up onto the edge of the pool and sat with Lot for a few minutes. I was less worried now. I knew that Lot wouldn't tell Hannah anything now that I had promised to give her ten thousand baht. When Hannah came back to me and started drying herself with her towel, she said, "She is such a lovely girl, so friendly."

"Where is she from?" I pretended not to know.

"She's from Thailand, obviously. She actually works in a bar across the road."

Back in our hotel room, I lay on the sofa, kept my eyes closed and repeatedly moaned about my terrible headache. I told Hannah that I was in no mood for going out for dinner, so we ordered room service. Everything was going perfectly. I had no intention of giving any money to Lot. Hannah and I could just stay in the safety of our room for the rest of the night and get a taxi straight to the airport tomorrow, so there would be no way for Lot to get to us. That was my hope anyway, but shortly after dinner, while I was lying on the sofa again, Hannah grabbed her purse off the coffee table and announced, "I'm gonna go to 7eleven to buy some stuff – snacks and maybe a beer or two. Do you want anything?"

I sat up quickly and said, "I'll go. You stay here."

"Don't be ridiculous," she said. "You're sick. Stay here and rest. Anyway, I told Lot I would pop into her bar to say hello. Maybe I'll have one drink there."

I couldn't let that happen.

"Call the reception," I suggested desperately. "Maybe they can bring up some snacks and beer."

"Chris, 7eleven is just across the road. I'll be back before you know it."

"I'm not letting you go out on your own in Bangkok at night. I'll go with you."

"You're being ridiculous," Hannah said, but I was already at the door putting on my flip flops.

In the elevator, I told Hannah, "Let's just say hello to your friend and then go to 7eleven quickly."

Hannah agreed. When we arrived at the bar, Lot welcomed Hannah very warmly. She took hold of Hannah's hand and led her to a seat at the bar. Hannah turned to me and said, "I guess we are having a drink."

She could see that I was not happy.

"Just a quick one," she added. "Five minutes max."

Hannah ordered a beer. I would have loved a beer too (God knows I needed one!) but I was still pretending to have the world's worst headache. I had to make do with a mineral water.

It wasn't even ten PM yet so the bar was very quiet. Lot sat with us, five other Thai women stood in the entrance trying to attract customers, and an older white guy sat a few stools down from us. While Hannah and Lot were talking happily, the falang rudely interrupted them and said to Hannah, "I am surprised to see a young couple in this kind of bar."

"And what do you mean by 'this kind of bar'?" Hannah asked.

The falang laughed and looked away, as he took a big

drink from his beer. Hannah turned back to Lot and they continued chatting without further interruption. Hannah's quick drink turned into a thirty-minute chat with her new Thai friend. Lot was being very friendly and charming, but I could see that it was all an act – the fake laugh, the fake compliments, typical bargirl stuff. Lot taught Hannah some basic Thai expressions and they even took some pictures together. Lot was surprised to hear that we were newlyweds on our honeymoon.

"I thought you only boyfriend and girlfriend," she said, laughing.

Towards the end of her beer, Hannah excused herself and went to use the bathroom in the back. As soon as she was out of sight, Lot turned to me and said, "Well?"

I took out ten thousand baht from my wallet, and before I handed it over, I whispered in a stern voice, "Don't say anything to my wife and don't show her the pictures."

Lot snapped the money out of my hand and shoved it into her pocket. No 'thank you', nothing, not even a smile or a nod of acknowledgement. In fact, I think I saw a hint of disgust on her face. Perhaps she was angry that I hadn't told her that Hannah was my wife. Or perhaps she hated me for not helping her 'sick mother' all those years ago.

I used the bathroom after Hannah, and when I came back

to my seat I saw two falangs come into the bar and sit in the corner. Two of the Thai girls sat with them and they were all over each other. The penny finally seemed to drop for Hannah. She realized what the drunken falang meant by 'this kind of bar'. Hannah suddenly looked uncomfortable. She quickly finished her beer and paid the bill. Hannah was in a rush to get out of the bar, but she still took the time to hold Lot's hand and thank her sincerely for her kindness. I could see that Hannah really appreciated the chance to spend time with a local person. They hugged each other and Lot wished us good luck on the rest of our travels.

I felt an incredible sense of relief when we left the bar and walked into the cool air-conditioned 7eleven. It was finally all over. Lot was dealt with and I could now start enjoying our honeymoon.

"Do men pay those women to go with them?" Hannah asked me, as she looked through the snack section.

"I guess so. This area is kind of famous for that kind of bar," I said. "That's why I said I fucked up when I booked this hotel."

"So Lot is a kind of prostitute? Poor girl."

Hannah was surprised to see me grab four large bottles of beer.

"What about your headache?" she asked.

"It's getting better."

I needed a few drinks to celebrate the end of the Lot nightmare.

The next morning we both woke up with a mild hangover. We would have loved to have slept more but we had a flight to Phuket to catch. When we were packed and ready to leave, I stood at the door with our bags and waited for Hannah. She placed her small bag on the dining table and double checked that she had everything – passports, flight tickets, money, phone, phone charger, laptop, et cetera. When she was looking through her purse, she unfolded a small piece of paper.

"Remind me to email Lot tonight," she said.

I was stunned.

"What are you talking about? Email her about what?"

"We took some photos together in the bar last night," Hannah said, putting the small piece of paper back in her purse. "She gave me her email so that I can send her on the photos."

I knew that if Hannah and Lot became email buddies, there would always be a possibility that Hannah would find out about me and Lot, and she might even see the pictures of us in bed together. I had no idea how Hannah would react if she knew that I had been with a prostitute, and I didn't want to find out.

Fortunately, Hannah did one final sweep of our hotel suite to make sure that we hadn't forgotten anything, and then she went into the bathroom. I took this chance to open up her purse and take the piece of paper with Lot's email address. I ripped it up and threw it in the trash can. Goodbye Lot. Only after I disposed of the paper did I start to wonder about Lot's intentions. Did she give Hannah her email address with the intention of telling her everything about us? Perhaps she planned to email me and ask me for more money, and if I didn't, she would threaten to send the photos of us in bed to Hannah. I would probably end up sending her money for years. Lot was a clever girl if that was really her plan.

When we were checking out of the hotel, we inquired about a taxi to the airport. The staff quoted us eight hundred baht. I knew that if we walked the one hundred meters to the main road we would be able to hail down a taxi and negotiate a fare for half that. So, we put on our backpacks and headed to Sukhumvit Road. We passed Lot's bar on the way. It was noon so of course the bar was closed. Surprisingly, it wasn't easy to hail down a taxi this time. We stood at the side of the road for several minutes without any luck. Finally, a taxi stopped for us and the driver quoted us a fare of six hundred baht.

"Just take it, Chris," Hannah said, sounding tired. "At least it's cheaper than what the hotel quoted."

I helped lift Hannah's backpack into the trunk, and then she sat in the taxi first. While I was placing my backpack in the trunk, I heard an unusually high voice call out, "Chris".

I was horrified to see a ladyboy I knew called Apple walk towards me. I slept with her six years ago. That night I was walking around Nana Plaza, tipsy and feeling adventurous, so I decided to go with a ladyboy. We spent a second night together a few days later. Now she was standing right in front of me. I was amazed that she remembered my name after all these years. She didn't notice my wife in the back seat of the taxi.

"You back?" Apple said, sounding very happy. "Why you not come look for me in Nana? I want stay with you again."

I slammed the trunk shut and jumped into the back seat before Apple could say anything else incriminating. But it was already too late. Hannah gave me a look that could kill.

"A ladyboy?" she asked, disgusted.

The honeymoon was ruined. Hannah barely spoke to me for the next ten days, and even after that things were really awkward between us. Things got back to normal by the time we reached Bali, and fortunately we are still happily married, but every time someone mentions Thailand around her, Hannah remembers

Apple the ladyboy and she gives me the silent treatment for a few days.

Trouble in Phuket

My friend (Katie) and I went on a two-week trip around Thailand – ten days of island hopping down south and four days of shopping and site seeing in Bangkok. During our last night in Phuket, we went out for a few drinks on Bangla Road. Katie paid fifty baht to have her picture taken with a ladyboy, and she even agreed to drink in some girly bars and play Connect Four and Jenga with the girls. I don't think she was even aware that the girls could be barfined by customers. She just thought they were regular bar staff. At about eleven o' clock, we were both tipsy and Katie wanted to go back to the hotel. We had to be up early the next morning for a long journey to our next destination, Ko Phangan. I walked Katie back to her room, and then I told her that I would go back out drinking on my own.

"But the bus is coming to pick us up at eight o' clock in the morning," Katie said, concerned that I would ruin our plans.

"I'll be fine," I said. "I just won't sleep tonight. I'll sleep on the bus."

"Have you even packed yet?"

"Oh shit! Good point," I admitted. "I'll pack now and then head out."

My room was right next to Katie's. I turned on the air conditioning in my room and started packing up my things very quickly. I heard the sound of water dropping onto the floor. I looked up and saw water dripping from the air conditioner. *This hotel is a shithole*, I said to myself. Half of the tiles in the bathroom were either cracked or chipped, the window didn't close properly, the TV had no sound, and now the air conditioner was dripping. But the hotel was cheap and the location was good.

As soon as I finished packing, I grabbed some extra cash and headed out. Earlier in the night I saw several women holding signs for a ping pong show near the top of Bangla Road. A few years ago, when I visited Thailand for the first time on my own, I had heard about the famous ping pong shows in Patpong, Bangkok. I had always avoided those kinds of places because I heard they were tourist traps. There were loads of stories online about how a guy ordered a beer for one hundred and fifty baht, and at the end when he tried to pay his bill, they charged him a thousand baht because of an unspecified entrance fee. But at the top of Bangla Road, women held signs that read, 'Ping Pong show. Cheap beer. No entrance fee. No hidden charges.' I decided to throw caution to the wind and finally experience one of these infamous shows.

As soon as I stepped onto Bangla Road, I saw the women holding signs for the ping pong show, but for some reason I felt too shy to approach them. *I'm not drunk enough yet*, I thought. *I need a few more beers.* I walked along Bangla Road and found a relatively quiet bar with empty seats facing out over the street. I ended up having four beers in that bar because I enjoyed people watching on Bangla Road so much. It was a fascinating stretch of road filled with tourists, street vendors and prostitutes. There were several older Thai women who walked up and down the street very slowly, looking for drunk or lonely-looking men to approach. Some ladyboys stood in groups and some stood alone, but they all looked bored or angry. It was late in the night and perhaps they hadn't found a customer yet.

The four beers had washed away my inhibitions. I was ready to go to a ping pong show, but first I had to get ready. I went to the bathroom and took out my wallet. I had over five thousand baht on me. I left five hundred baht in my wallet and stashed the rest in my left sock. That way, if the bar did try to scam me out of money, I could show them my wallet and explain that I could only pay five hundred baht. When I left the bar, I made a beeline for the women with the ping pong signs and asked one of them to lead the way. She brought me down a small side alley.

"There are no entrance fees or hidden charges, right?" I asked.

"Yes, mister. Only pay for beer," she said.

"And how much is beer?"

"Chang and Leo one hundred and fifty baht. Good price. Don't worry."

The woman led me through thick violet doorway curtains. She used her cardboard sign to make a gap in the curtains for me. Inside there was a small amphitheater with a stage at the front. There were three poles on the stage and the back walls were lined completely with mirrors. The woman led me quickly to a seat in the third row. Then she handed me a menu. The bar was extremely dark. The woman pulled out a flashlight to help me read the menu. I looked carefully to make sure there was no fine print. Satisfied but still cautious, I ordered a beer. The woman told my order to a waitress next to the stage and then she headed back to Bangla Road with her sign.

While I was waiting for my beer, I looked around the amphitheater. I had expected to see only a couple of old men in the audience, but I was surprised to see that more than half of the seats were filled. I was even more surprised to see that the audience was made up of people of all ages, and there were even a few Western couples. The ping pong show had transcended the sex industry and had become a popular tourist attraction. A beautiful young waitress brought me my beer and placed a bin (a small wooden container to hold bills) on my table. She held up a piece of paper and said, "This your bill for one beer. One hundred and fifty baht," and then she put the bill into the bin. .

The stage was completely empty. I asked the waitress, "When does the show start?"

"Dancing start soon, then show."

Her answer was frustratingly vague. A few minutes later, three young Thai women in pink bikinis got on the stage and started dancing. I had no interest in watching them dance. I guess I had been to too many Go-go bars over the years. I drank my beer impatiently. Fifteen minutes later, I raised my hand and signaled to the waitress that I wanted one more beer. When she brought it, I asked her again, "What time does the show start?"

"Five minutes, I think," she answered unconvincingly.

Fifteen minutes of more dancing and I needed a new beer.

"Will it start soon?" I asked the waitress.

"Yes, it start now."

I decided that if the show didn't start by the time I finished this beer, I would pay my bill and leave.

Half way through my third beer, the music stopped and the dancers left the stage. A Thai woman in her late thirties, also wearing a pink bikini, walked slowly onto the stage. Apart from having fifteen years on the other women, she wore much thicker make up and she had a lot of flab around her belly. Her dancing days were long behind her. She sat down on the stage and pulled her bikini bottom to one side. Only at this moment did I notice that she was holding two ping pong balls in her right hand. She stuck one of them into her vagina and adjusted her position slightly to face one of the dancers who was now standing in front of the first row. Without any hint of ceremony or delay, she grimaced slightly and the ball came flying out of her vagina. The dancer had to dive to her left to catch it. The crowd gasped in amazement and then gave a quick round of applause, me included. The ping pong woman fired the next ball, only this time her aim was much better and the dancer was able to catch it easily. The ping pong woman got the two balls back, and this time she fired them into the audience. A man caught one of the balls, but the other ball fell short and hit an empty seat. I felt fortunate that she didn't aim in my direction.

I thought the dancer would hand the balls back to the ping

pong woman to repeat the same feat in different positions, perhaps hitting different targets, but the balls were discarded and the dancer handed the woman three darts instead. *Jesus! Darts!* I thought.

The dancer held up a balloon, and the ping pong woman fired a dart out of her vagina and burst the balloon in one go. The ping pong woman had perfect aim – three balloons with three darts. We were only three minutes into the show and already she had fired ping pong balls and darts, so I wondered where the show was going. *What will she fire out of her vagina next?* I could never have guessed what I was about to witness.

The dancer carried a small fish bowl containing two gold fish onto the stage. She placed the fish bowl on the ground and used a net to scoop out the two little fish. The ping pong woman put both fish into her vagina and then squatted over the fishbowl. She stayed in this position for a full minute, and then she released one of the fish. It came flying through the air and landed in the fishbowl with a plop! The second fish came out a few seconds later. The audience clapped in appreciation and amazement. I was stunned that the woman was sticking living things up her vagina, but I was also critical of her display. The firing of the ping pong balls and the darts was impressive because her aim was good and she was somehow able to generate enough power in her vagina to shoot these items into the air. But the fish trick was no trick at all. She just stuck the fish up her vagina and let them fall out. It was shocking to see, but in some ways it was underwhelming.

I fully expected the show to end at this point and for the dancers to return to the stage and start gyrating around the poles again. But actually the show had only just begun. Next, the ping pong woman was handed a small cage with a hamster inside. She didn't hesitate. She stuck the hamster up her vagina and then walked from one side of the stage to the other, waving at the audience and blowing kisses. Then the dancer lay down in the middle of the stage and the ping pong woman squatted over her. The hamster came flying through the air like a sky diver. The dancer caught it with two hands. A huge round of applause filled the room again. Then a different dancer carried another fishbowl onto the stage, but this fishbowl didn't contain any water. I squinted and strained my eyes to see what was inside. I was shocked to see a snake coiled up at the bottom of the bowl. I could barely watch as the ping pong woman put the snake inside her body, waited and then let it drop into the fishbowl. Horrific! But fascinating! *Surely that was the grand finale,* I thought, but I was wrong again. For the grand finale, one of the dancers carried a bird cage onto the stage. I couldn't make out the colors of the bird clearly because the lights on the stage were dim, but it was a small bird and I could see its head move as the dancer handed it carefully to the ping pong woman with two hands. After the bird disappeared up the woman's vagina, she bowed to the audience and then lay down on the stage. She opened her legs very slowly. The dancers asked the audience to join them in counting down from five. I stayed quiet, but the rest of the audience counted loudly and slowly, "Five...four...three...two..." and at the very moment they said "one", the bird appeared from between the woman's legs and went soaring up through the air. All eyes followed this tiny bird as it flew above the audience in quick circles for a couple of seconds, before it flew up above the lights and hid in a dark corner. By the time we all looked back at the ping pong woman, she was already walking off the stage and it was too late to give her a final round of applause.

"Tip for the woman in show."

I looked up and saw a waitress holding out a small basket.

"Tip for the woman in show," she repeated.

I grabbed a handful of coins from my pocket – about one hundred baht worth – and dropped them into the basket. I watched the ping pong woman closely. When she came down from the stage, she stood alone and sipped on a glass of beer. She turned away from the audience and faced the toilets. The dancers and waitresses were standing in their own groups, chatting together, but nobody talked to the ping pong woman. Suddenly I was very attracted to her. What I had seen her do on stage would be a turn-off if I was sober, but now that I was drunk, it kind of turned me on. And I felt sorry for her because she looked so lonely and vulnerable. I considered calling a waitress over and inquiring about whether the ping pong woman could be barfined. *Am I really gonna do this?* I asked myself. *Do I really want to go with a woman who just stuck a snake up her vagina?*

While most of the audience stood up and started to leave, I nursed my last beer and thought seriously about whether I should make a move for the ping pong woman. *I'll never have a chance to be with a woman like that again.* I thought. *I'll regret it if I don't try.* Then I heard a man's voice come out of the speakers, "Next show in half hour".

The ping pong woman was due back on stage in thirty minutes, and then probably thirty minutes after that again. God knows how many shows she did every night. I figured she was simply too busy to go with customers, so I gave up on her. I finished my beer and called over a waitress to pay my bill. She took out my three bills from the bin and she looked at them closely with a flashlight.

"Four hundred and fifty baht," she said, playfully flashing the light in my eyes for half a second.

I laughed and I felt great that nobody was trying to rip me off. I handed the girl five hundred baht and told her to keep the change. As soon as I got out of the bar, I took the rest of my money out from my sock.

It was still kind of early, only about one AM. All the bars on Bangla Road were still open and the place was buzzing. When I left Katie in the hotel, I had planned to drink alone and stay alone, but the ping pong woman had stirred something inside me, and now I was determined to find a woman. I hopped from girly bar to girly bar, but none of the girls took my fancy. When some of the bars started to close and the streets started to empty, I sat on the steps of a 7eleven and drank water. I hoped that a beautiful woman would approach me, but I only attracted ladyboys. I wandered along Beach Road and Second Road for over an hour. *Anyone will do now*, I thought. *Don't be picky. The night is almost over.* But incredibly there were no women around. All the bars were closed and the only people on the streets were drunk falangs, ladyboys and tuk-tuk drivers. I needed food. I sat down for a burger in McDonalds and when I finished it was already bright outside. It was nearly six AM. I decided to walk along Bangla Road one last time in search of a woman. If I couldn't find one this time, I would go back to my hotel and sleep for an hour before the journey to Ko Phangan.

Bangla Road was almost deserted, but there were a couple of old women with food carts selling rice and small plastic bags of papaya salad and other Thai dishes. There were buildings with cheap rooms down some of the side streets, so I guessed that's where their customers were coming from. I had almost reached the top of Bangla Road when I heard a voice call out, "Hey, mister."

I looked around but couldn't see anyone.

"Mister, over here."

I saw two Thai women standing together half way down a side street to my right. I pointed at myself and said, "Me?"

"Yes, you. Come."

As I got closer, I saw that the woman who called me over was in her early forties and her friend was almost twenty years younger.

"You look for woman?" the older one asked me.

"Maybe."

"Me and my friend want go with you."

I looked at them both and considered the proposition. The younger one had a pretty face, but she was too skinny – nothing but skin and bones. The older one was plain looking and it looked like she had been around the block a few too many times, but she was busty. I wasn't very keen on either of them but I was running out of time. I figured if I could negotiate a good deal, I'd go for it.

48

We agreed on a fee of seven hundred and fifty baht each, and three hundred baht for a room. I was surprised that they agreed to such a low fee, but then again it was six AM in the morning and I was the only falang on Bangla Road.

The two women led me to an old rundown building at the end of the side street. I paid three hundred baht to use a room for an hour. The two women led me up to the second floor. Instead of being excited about having a threesome, I felt uneasy because I didn't really want to be there. I was not attracted to either woman, yet here I was about to pay to have sex with them. It didn't feel right. We entered the room, left our shoes at the door and the older woman locked the door behind us. She said something to the younger one and they both started undressing. Before they took anything off, I said, "Wait, wait. Don't take your clothes off. I'm sorry, but I changed my mind. I don't want to go through with this."

The younger one looked confused. I guess she wasn't good at English. The older one understood what I had said and she was pissed off.

"What you talk about?" she started yelling. "You say downstairs you want go with both of us."

"I know, I'm sorry," I said. "I made a mistake. I'll go now."

I tried to walk to the door, but the older one stood in my way.

"Fine, go," she said. "But first you must pay. Seven hundred and fifty baht each."

"Pay? Pay for what? We didn't do anything."

"You crazy?" she screamed at me, and she bent down to pick up one of her shoes. There was a four-inch heel on the shoe, so it was a weapon.

"We come room with you. You say you pay us, so pay us."

She looked at me with intense anger in her eyes, breathing heavily and loudly through her nose, holding her shoe in her right hand up above her head. This woman was scary. She kept staring at me with this vicious look, and it felt like if I stared back at her, she would pounce and attack me wildly. I turned to the younger woman and said softly, "I'm sorry about this. You are lovely and really pretty, but I'm tired and I just want to go back to my room."

She looked very calm and kind, but she probably didn't understand a word I was saying. I looked back at the older one.

"I really am sorry," I said.

"You not pay?" she asked.

"I will not pay."

"Then you wait here. I call my friend. He come here and he make you pay."

"Okay. Whatever," I said, trying to play it cool.

I sat down at the edge of the bed while she made a phone call. She talked on the phone in Thai for a few minutes. I looked over at the younger one. She looked worried, but I wasn't sure who she was worried for. The older one hung up the phone and said to me, "My friend come now. He be here in five minutes. You can tell him why you not want to pay."

"Fine," I said.

I walked over to the window and looked out onto the side street. There were a few Thai people walking around and two men sitting on bikes smoking cigarettes. The older woman spoke frantically to her friend in Thai, and then she turned to me and asked, "Why you no pay? You bad man."

"I'm sorry. I cannot pay," I said. "We didn't do anything, and I already paid three hundred baht for the room."

This seemed to make her even angrier. She stepped closer to me and shook her shoe frantically in the air.

"You pay the room money to hotel, not to us," she yelled. "Why you talk about room money?"

I looked out the window again. Nobody was coming yet, but I expected to see a motorbike speed down the side alley and pull up outside the hotel at any minute. I knew that there was a strong possibility that she was bluffing about her friend, but I didn't want to stay to find out. I wanted to get out of there quickly.

The quickest way out of the situation would have been to pay the girls, but my drunken stubbornness wouldn't let me do that, even though I had plenty of money in my wallet. My only other option was to do a runner. I looked at them both in the eyes and said one more time, "I really am sorry".

Then I marched passed the older one. She tried to grab my arm but I shrugged it off and ran to the front door. As I bent down to pick up my shoes, she swung with all her mite and struck me in the neck with the heel of her shoe.

"Fuck!" I screamed out in pain, but I didn't turn back. I sprinted out of the room in my bare feet.

The older one screamed something out the door, but surprisingly she didn't follow me. Fortunately, the younger one kept out of the whole thing. If she had gotten involved, it wouldn't have been so easy for me to escape. I put on my shoes, walked out of the hotel quickly and then ran towards Bangla Road.

On my way back to my hotel, I felt the part of my neck where the high heel had struck. I was lucky to get away with a scratch. It was exciting to do a runner, but I immediately felt terrible about what I had done. Even though the older one had attacked me, I didn't blame her for it. I had promised her and her friend money, followed them to a hotel room and then backed out of our deal at the very last second. I should have paid them something. The younger one didn't seem very bothered by it all because she probably got a lot of customers and made a lot of money throughout the night. But the older one seemed desperate. She might have really needed that money to buy food or pay her bills. I was in the wrong, no doubt.

I thought I could forget about my weird final night in Phuket and get half an hour of much needed sleep before heading to Ko Phangan, but as I approached my hotel room, I realized that my room key was not in either of my pockets. I couldn't remember the last time I saw it. *Perhaps I left it in the room*, I thought. I went down to the reception area and fortunately the hotel owner – a middle aged Thai man – was already awake.

"I'm sorry, but I think I left my key in my room," I said. "Could you help me?"

He sighed deeply. Without saying anything to me, he grabbed a large key ring with dozens of keys on it, and stomped around the reception desk and up the stairs. With a quick flick of his wrist, he signaled for me to follow him. When he let me into my room, I started looking for the key under the bedclothes, under the bed, in my bag, in the bathroom and so on. I was tired now so I gave up quickly. I turned to the hotel owner and said, "I've lost the key."

He rolled his eyes at me and said, "Okay, you pay one

thousand baht for new key."

"One thousand baht?" I asked, shocked. "No, come on. That's too much."

"One thousand baht!"

I figured it probably cost forty baht to get a new key copied. One thousand baht was ridiculous. The room was only five hundred baht a night.

"I'm not paying one thousand baht," I said. "No way."

"One thousand baht for new key! You lost it, you pay," he shouted.

"Why should I?" I exploded. "This room is a shithole. The tiles in the bathroom are all fucked, the air conditioner leaks, the TV has no sound."

Out of nowhere, the hotel owner ran towards me and punched me in the face full force.

"I know what you do," he screamed viciously in my face. "You stay out all night and go with women in bars. I know what falang do. Now pay one thousand baht for new key or I call police."

I was stunned. The man was much shorter, skinnier and older than me. I could have beat him up easily, but fortunately I had enough sense not to hit back. *Jai yen. Jai yen*, I told myself, which is Thai for 'stay calm', 'don't get angry' or more literally 'cool heart'. I had heard so many tales of caution about not getting into arguments or fights with Thai people because the falang will always be blamed. I knew that if I hit him back he could call the police and I'd probably end up paying a hefty fine. I had to swallow my pride on this one. I took out my wallet and handed him a thousand baht. He snapped it out of my hand with disdain.

As soon as the hotel owner left my room, I went to knock on Katie's door. She answered her door surprisingly quickly. Before I could say anything, she said, "I heard everything. Are you okay? Your eye is red."

"Yeah, I'm okay," I said. "Do you wanna get a cup of coffee before the bus comes to pick us up?"

"Sure. You can tell me all about what you got up to last night."

We grabbed our bags and checked out of the hotel. In a nearby cafe, I told Katie about my night. I left out the part about being attacked by a woman with a high heel, and I focused mainly on the ping pong show and all the different animals involved. She was highly amused by it all. It was an eventful night in Phuket. I was lucky to be leaving with just a scratch on my neck and a black eye.

Love Gone Wrong

A few years ago, my wife and I decided to travel to Thailand for ten days. Our close friend had recently opened a restaurant in Phuket, so we wanted to visit him. We had never travelled outside of Europe before. This was a big trip for us. We went to a doctor a couple of months in advance and got all the recommended jabs. We packed malaria tablets, half a dozen bottles of mosquito spray, and a sizeable first aid kit to keep us safe in exotic Thailand. Leaving our two teenage sons behind, my wife and I flew from London Heathrow to Phuket via Bangkok. The journey took a lot out of us. We weren't used to such long flights. Our friend, Colin, was there to meet us at the Arrival Gate in Phuket Airport. The first thing I noticed about Colin was that he had lost a lot of weight since I last saw him two years ago. But there was no chance of me not recognizing Colin because we he was a very tall, very bald lad with an unusually large and pointed nose. You couldn't miss him, no matter how much weight he lost. Both my wife and I hugged Colin warmly. He was one of our closest friends, and we became particularly close when Colin's wife died in a car accident four years ago. My wife and I tried to support Colin as much as we could, but he felt lost without his late wife. Loneliness started to get the better of him, which was probably one of the reasons he decided to come to Thailand to start a new life.

Colin had a taxi waiting for us. Even during the few minutes it took to walk to the taxi and load our luggage in the trunk, I could feel the heat of Phuket drain me. The sweat started pouring down my forehead. Without any delays, we jumped in the taxi and headed straight for our hotel in Patong. Colin sat in the front seat and turned around to speak with us. He was full of life and excited to see familiar faces, but my wife and I were only fit for bed.

"How was the flight?" he asked my wife.

"Long. Never again," she moaned.

"You'll feel better after a power nap, or do you want to eat something first?"

"We'll need to sleep first," I said.

Colin helped us check in to our hotel and then he gave me simple directions to his restaurant.

"Come as soon as you wake up and I'll give you a good

feed," he said. "If you have trouble finding the restaurant, find a phone and call me."

Colin handed us his business card and left.

The view from our hotel was beautiful. We could see right along Patong beach and over the ocean. There was a veranda with a small table and two chairs.

"This almost makes up for the long flight," my wife said, impressed by the view and the veranda. "It'll be nice at night with a book and a glass of wine."

My wife and I went to bed at 3 PM. We planned to have a quick nap, but we eventually woke up at around 9 PM.

It was easy to find Colin's restaurant. Our hotel was located on the beach front, and his restaurant was located on the second road in from the beach, almost directly behind our hotel. Colin's restaurant was smaller than I had expected. There were only eight tables, but it was a busy spot. There was only one table free when we arrived. All the customers were foreigners. The only Thai people we could see were the staff. Colin wasn't there when we arrived so the waitress handed us two menus and treated us like normal customers. It was a large menu, with dozens of Western and Thai dishes. My wife and I were shocked by the prices. Some of the meals were only three pounds, and the beer was only about two pounds.

"How does he make money?" my wife asked me.

"The overheads must be very low," I said.

I ordered fried rice and my wife ordered a steak, and we got a couple of beers too – two bottles of Chang, I think it was called. While we were waiting for our food, I saw Colin walk into the bar with a huge bag of ice over his shoulder.

"You found the place alright?" he said, as he walked past.

Colin handed the bag of ice to one of the waiters before he came to sit with us.

"Did you have a nice nap?" he asked us.

"I'm not sure I would call it a nap," I said. "We slept for six hours."

"You have a lovely restaurant here," my wife complimented Colin. "It's so busy even though it's quite late."

"Yeah, Bangla Road is near here, so we stay busy until about 11."

"What is Bangla Road?" my wife asked.

"You guys don't know about Bangla Road?"

"No, never heard of it," I said. "What is it?"

"Let's go together after you have finished your meal, and you can see it for yourself," Colin said, with a big grin on his face. "It's fun to walk down Bangla Road with newbies and see the look on their faces."

My wife and I were very curious. We ate our meals faster than normal and finished our beers. We were ready for Bangla Road.

We followed Colin along the street. I'm not sure what my wife thought, but even the walk towards Bangla Road was kind of shocking to me. In the space of about two hundred meters, we passed half a dozen massage shops with scantily clad young women waiting outside looking for customers. They didn't bother me or my wife because we were walking hand in hand, but I overheard them say, "Sexy massage, good price for you," to one young man. I also noticed a lot of tall women standing in dark alleys waiting for customers. Colin later told me that they were ladyboys.

As we approached Bangla Road, I noticed dozens of Thai men standing at the side of the road.

"What are they doing?" I asked Colin.

"They are tuk-tuk drivers," he explained. "Bangla Road is the busiest place in Patong, so tuk-tuk drivers wait at both ends for customers."

When my wife and I finally stepped onto Bangla Road, we were blown away. The road was lined either side with hundreds of bars and clubs, each with its own huge, impossibly bright neon sign. They were all piled on top of each other, each one more colorful than the next. They were hideous. The neon lights were blinding and the music was deafening. The dance music from the first bar on my left was smashing against my ears so I quickened my step to get out of earshot, but there was no escape because the music in the next bar was just as loud. The crowds astonished me too. The area around our hotel and Colin's restaurant was not very busy, but this road was teeming with people. There were hundreds of people walking up and down the street at any one time. The road was long and wide, so there was always enough space to walk into, but it amazed me how much busier it was compared to other roads we had seen in Phuket.

"What kind of bars and clubs are these?" my wife asked Colin.

"Some are just normal bars and normal clubs, but most of the bars have bar girls that customers can go with if they pay the bar 500 baht," Colin explained.

There seemed to be hundreds of attractive Thai women in sexy, colorful uniforms standing in the middle of the road holding cardboard signs that read 'Buy 1 beer get 1 beer free' or 'Beer 80 baht', or something else to attract the tourists into their bar. There were also girls with no signs, and they used their free hands to grab our arms and try to physically drag us into their bar.

"Is this a redlight district?" my wife asked Colin.

"Kind of," he answered.

"So why are there families?" she asked.

She was right. There were several families with young children walking along the street. It looked like they were on a family vacation and taking a leisurely stroll around town. I could never imagine bringing young children to such a place. There were also couples and groups of young Western women walking along the street, looking up at the neon signs, talking with the girls holding signs, and taking pictures of the various oddities around the place. Bangla Road seemed to be a tourist attraction that appealed to all kinds of tourists, not just sex tourists.

Half way up the road to our right, we saw a group of ladyboys standing outside a bar. They were posing for pictures. My wife walked up to a tall, beautiful ladyboy and asked if she could take a picture.

"Yes, of course," the ladyboy replied, in a high squeaky voice. "500 baht."

"500 baht?" my wife gasped. "For a picture? No thank you."

Colin led us to a relatively quiet part of Bangla Road, where there were dozens of open bars grouped together. He brought us into an empty bar. There were four young women standing behind the bar and one middle-aged Thai woman sitting on a stool looking at her phone. We sat down and ordered three beers. The girls left us alone.

"Who is the older lady sitting at the bar?" my wife asked Colin. "The owner?"

"No, she is probably the Mamasan," Colin answered. "She manages the girls and the money."

"So you reckon all these girls go with customers for money?" I asked, shocked at the scale of prostitution in the area.

"Yes, they are all available. Even the Mamasan probably goes with customers sometimes."

"Do you come here often?" my wife asked Colin, throwing him a judgmental look.

"From time to time," Colin answered, a little awkwardly. "Sometimes my customers ask me to come here with them for a drink. And anyway, a lot of people come here to drink and have a good time, without any intention of going with the girls."

While Colin was talking, one of the girls behind the bar smiled at me sweetly. I smiled back. This girl was a little shorter than the other three girls, and she had a straight-cut fringe that reached down to her eyes. She had thick creamy brown lips and a cute round face. There was nothing out of the ordinary about her clothes; she was wearing light denim jeans and a tight white T-shirt. She looked like a normal bar tender or waitress to me. During the next few minutes we made eye contact a few times. It was very exciting. Then she walked towards me with something in her hand.

"You want play Connect Four with me?" she asked, placing a Connect Four set on the bar.

That was the last question I was expecting. My wife and I looked at Colin for an explanation.

"What's going on?" I asked.

"In these kinds of bars, the girls often play Connect Four or Jenga," Colin explained, clearly amused by the confused look on our faces.

"Why?" my wife asked.

"I guess it helps break the ice with the customers."

I agreed to play Connect Four with this lovely young woman who I had been catching sneaky glimpses at for the past few minutes.

"What's your name?" I asked.

"My name Bean," she said. "What your name?"

"My name is Ken."

"Ken, you are red color. You go first."

Colin and my wife watched our game keenly. Even though I went first, Bean won easily. Colin and my wife gave Bean a cheerful high-five when she beat me. We were all warming to Bean. She was lovely.

"One more time," I said to her. "I know where I went wrong.

I should focus more on the middle."

"Okay, one more time, no problem," she agreed, setting up the Connect Four set again. "But this time if I win, you buy me beer."

"And if I win?"

"You no win," she said, smiling at me very cutely.

"But if I win?" I said, smiling back.

"If you win, I buy you beer too, or kiss on the cheek. You choose. But you not win."

This time Bean went first. It was a close game, but she won in the end and I bought her a beer. Bean sat and talked with the three of us. We all got on great with her. Her English was not great, but she had us all in stitches at times. My wife noticed a small tattoo of a bike on her ankle. It looked like a kid's drawing. Bean said it was a picture of a bike her mom gave her on her tenth birthday. My wife thought it was the sweetest thing she ever heard.

After a couple of beers, Colin said it was time for him to go home to bed, but my wife and I stayed with Bean for a while. She gave us good advice about what Thai food we should try and about some beautiful less-known beaches around Phuket. I had four beers, while my wife nursed the same beer the whole night. Now that I was a little tipsy, I started asking Bean about how she ended up working in this kind of bar.

"I no work here long time," she said, now looking a little sad. "This only second month here. I no want to work this kind of place, but my momma and papa get very sick recently. Hospital very expensive in Thailand. I work in clothes store before, but money not enough so I come here. Please understand. Please don't think I am bad girl."

Both my wife and I felt sorry for Bean when we heard about her struggles. We could see the sadness in her eyes. When my wife and I were ready to call it a night, we paid our bill and gave Bean a one-thousand-baht-tip to put towards taking care of her parents. Bean was sad to see us leave and she made us promise that we would come back to see her the following night, even if it was just to say hello.

I'm not sure if it was because of the jetlag or because of Bean, but I couldn't fall asleep that night. I lay awake next to my wife and thought about lovely, beautiful Bean. I missed her already. The next day my wife and I woke up late and went straight to Colin's restaurant for lunch. I couldn't stop thinking about Bean and I kept looking out at the street in the hope of seeing her walk by. It seems like I wasn't the only one thinking about her, because over lunch my wife said, "We must go to see Bean again tonight." I was delighted.

My wife and I told Colin about how fond we were of Bean,

and we asked him about her situation.

"Is she really a prostitute?" my wife asked.

"She's a bir girl," Colin replied.

"What's the difference?" she asked.

"I'm not sure there is a difference."

"How can her parents let her go with men for money like that?"

"Her parents probably live on a farm up in north Thailand. They don't know, or they don't want to know, what their daughter is doing for money."

My wife and I were confused. Bean looked kind and pure, and we already considered her our friend. We found it hard to believe that she sold her body for money.

Colin rented a taxi for the whole day to show us around Phuket. He brought us to a beautiful place called Karen beach after lunch, and then we went to a shopping mall in Phuket town. It was great to see different sides of the island, but all I could think about was seeing Bean again that night. I was counting down the hours. For dinner, Colin brought us to a seafood restaurant near our hotel. After we ate, he said he had to go take care of his restaurant for a few hours. My wife and I were at a loose end so we decided to go have a beer with Bean. There were two other male customers in the bar when we got there, but she sat with us and talked with us the whole time. She was as lovely as the night before, only this time I noticed that she was more flirtatious. She kept saying how handsome and kind I was, and how beautiful and sexy my wife was. At first I just thought she was being playful, but then I started to think that perhaps she wanted to come back to our hotel room with us. It was all very exciting for me, but I could see that my wife was starting to feel uncomfortable. Halfway through my second beer, my wife said that she was tired and wanted to go back to the hotel.

"I'm not even halfway through my beer," I protested.

"Drink up," she said.

I pleaded with my wife, perhaps a little too much, to stay for one more beer. She refused. My wife is a very perceptive woman, and she must have seen that I had developed feelings for Bean. I was staring at her too much, smiling at her too brightly, and finding excuses to touch her hand or arm. The next day my wife told me that she didn't want to go to Bean's bar again. I played it cool and didn't argue with her.

My wife and I enjoyed the rest of our trip in Phuket, and on our last night we agreed that we should drop by Bean's bar to say goodbye to her quickly. Bean looked very happy to see us, but when we told her that it was our last night in Phuket, her face dropped. Tears came to her eyes when we said goodbye to her. For whatever reason, I felt a strong bond with her; we just clicked from the first time we played Connect Four together. On the flight back to England, I couldn't help wonder what it would be like to go back to Phuket without my wife. I would be able to go talk with Bean on my own and perhaps even meet her outside of the bar. It was a thrilling thought, and by the time our plane landed in Heathrow, I had a simple plan to make it happen.

Soon after we returned to England, my mates and I started to discuss our annual golfing trip. We usually got cheap flights and headed off to Spain, Portugal or Ireland, but this time I suggested we try Thailand. All three of my mates were against the idea because they thought the flight would be too long and too expensive for a one-week golfing trip. I explained that food and drink is very cheap in Thailand, so golf would probably be cheap too. My mates were friends with Colin. I pointed out that we could catch up with him on the trip too. They took some convincing, but eventually they agreed that it would be fun to go somewhere far afield for once. When I told my wife that we were planning to go to Phuket for our golf trip, she didn't look too pleased, but she didn't oppose it either.

We flew into Phuket in the evening. Colin was at the airport to welcome us. It had only been four months since I had last seen him. We got two taxis to the same hotel that my wife and I had stayed in. Shortly after we checked in, my mates went to Colin's restaurant for dinner, but I told them I wanted to have a walk around Patong on my own. I told them I would look for them on Bangla Road later. Once my mates were out of sight, I made a beeline for Bean's bar. As I walked up Bangla Road, I didn't pay the slightest bit of notice to all the ladyboys or freelancers. I rushed towards Bean's bar, and it was an amazing feeling when I saw her running towards me with open arms.

"Ken," she shouted out with joy. She remembered my name! "You're back?"

We hugged tightly.

"Yes, I am back. I'm so happy to see you."

"Me too. Where your wife?" she asked, looking around.

"My wife didn't come. I am here with my friends."

"Really?" Bean's face lit up when she heard this news. "You can have drink with me?"

I ordered a beer for myself and a lady drink for Bean. The lady drink was a small glass with a lot of ice and a small bit of coke and Jack Daniels. The lady drink was two hundred baht, twice as much as my beer. This time we didn't play Connect Four because Bean wanted to talk with me. She said she never forgot how sad she was the last time I left. She said she thought I was angry with her because we didn't visit her for the last five days of our trip.

"I wasn't angry with you," I assured Bean. "You remembered my name?"

"Of course. You special man. You so kind and nice to me. I never forget."

"How are your parents?" I asked her.

"You remember my parents?"

Bean was touched that I remembered her sick parents, but she looked sad and worried as soon she started talking about them.

"They still very sick," Bean said. "They take many medicine and go to hospital many time. Very expensive. I am worried I cannot help them anymore. Hospitals crazy expensive in Thailand."

Tears started pouring down Bean's face. I put my arm around her and patted her on her bare shoulder. Even in this sad moment, I couldn't help but be aroused by her dark, smooth skin.

Bean and I talked for hours. She told me more about her sick parents and we cried together. I told her that I had lost both my parents when I was around her age. We understood each other so well. My arm was now fixed around Bean, as she rested her head on my shoulder.

There were two falangs in the bar when I arrived, but they

both went off somewhere with a girl each. About forty minutes later, both of the girls came back to the bar without the falangs. When new customers came, the girls played Connect Four and Jenga with them. One of the girls went off with her second falang in the space of a couple of hours. I asked Bean about this.

"That girl name is Nung. She very popular."

"Do you go with customers every night too?" I asked Bean, afraid of what she might say.

"I'm sorry, Ken. I am bad girl," she said, lowering her head in shame. "I no want to do this job but I need money to help parents. Please understand."

"I understand," I said. "I'm sorry. I didn't mean to make you sad."

I asked Bean about her dream in life, and I was surprised to hear that it was quite a modest one.

"My dream is simple. I want study English and be English teacher."

I thought it was a great idea and very achievable. The more I talked with Bean, the more I realized that there was a lot I could do to help her, but first I decided to go back to my hotel before I got too drunk. I didn't want to make any rash decisions on the first night of my trip. It was amazing just to be able to talk with Bean freely and to hold her. When I went to the Mamasan to pay my bill,

I was surprised by the amount. It was more than I had expected, but I didn't question it in front of Bean. I didn't want her to think that I was tight. After I paid the bill, I handed Bean a one-thousand-baht tip. She didn't ask for it, or even hint at it, but I wanted to give it to her because I knew she must have been missing out on chances to earn money from other customers while she was talking with me. I kissed Bean on the cheek and hugged her warmly. I promised that I would come back the next night.

When I entered my hotel room, I saw a piece of paper on the floor. Somebody must have slid it under the door while I was out. It read, 'Ken, where did you go? We are going to Bangla Road now with Colin for a few beers. Colin is the only one with a phone, so call him if you want to join us. Charles.'

I gave Colin a quick ring from the phone in my hotel room to tell him that I was back at the hotel safely and getting ready for bed. Then I had a quick shower, and before I fell asleep I sent my wife a loving email, telling her how much I loved and missed her.

The next day my mates and I met downstairs at 9 AM for breakfast - dried scrambled eggs, thin and stale slices of toast, and cereal with strange tasting milk. My mates were quick to ask me about what happened to me the night before.

"I just walked around for a while and stopped at a random bar. The people were nice and there was a pool table so I stayed for a while. I got a bit drunk and lost track of the time."

"Bullshit!" my mate, Charles, said. "You met a girl."

"I did not," I insisted, but they teased me about it over breakfast and several times during our round of golf.

In the evening, we all went to Colin's restaurant. I ate quickly and made my excuses to leave.

"Why don't you let us see her?" Charles joked.

"I'm just going for a walk," I said, but I wasn't fooling anyone.

I headed straight for Bean's bar. I was surprised that she was not there when I arrived. The other three girls were there, two of whom were busy playing Connect Four with two falangs. I asked the Mamasan about Bean.

"She start work late today," she answered. "She come here soon. Don't worry. You very early today."

"Yes, I'm a little earlier than usual," I said, as I sat down on the stool and ordered a beer from the girl who didn't have a falang.

I wondered if she might try to talk with me, but she left me alone because she knew that I had only come to see Bean.

About forty minutes later, Bean arrived. When she saw me, she came to me with open arms. This time she gave me a big bear hug. It was a cute bear hug, I must say, especially the way she sank her face into my chest and let her long dark hair rest on my arms.

"Where have you been?" I asked.

"I talk with father on phone long time," she said, looking stressed and tired. "My mom go to hospital today morning. She very sick. Doctors worry about her. Maybe I need send more money soon."

I bought Bean a lady drink and she told me more about her parents. It was a sad story about how both her parents were diagnosed with cancer at the same time, and about how she, as the only child, was responsible for paying for all their treatment. Bean said she was worried and sad so she wanted to drink a lot. I must have bought her five lady drinks at two hundred baht a pop within an hour, but I was just happy that I could be there to comfort her.

Bean and I were getting on great. We sat close together at the bar. The biggest jump forward in our relationship was when Bean held my hand with interlocking fingers and rubbed my palm gently with her thumb. This was a huge step for us. Then the night took a strange turn when Colin suddenly turned up at the bar and handed me his phone. Bean walked over to the Mamasan to give me some privacy.

"There's a call for you," he said.

"Who is it?" I asked.

"See for yourself."

"Hello," I said into the phone.

"Hi Ken."

It was my wife.

"I know you are talking with Bean," she said, very composed, very calm.

I didn't deny it.

"Ken, finish your beer and then please go back to your hotel alone," my wife said, her voice now sounding less composed and very vulnerable. "I know you have developed strong feelings for Bean. Even when we were in Phuket together, I could see how much you liked her. Please don't throw our marriage away. Remember all the years we have spent together. Don't destroy our family. Think of our two kids."

"I won't do anything," I said, rather unconvincingly.

"Promise me you will open your email tomorrow at 4 PM," my wife said.

"Why?"

"Just promise me," she said, her voice quivering.

"Okay. Okay. I promise."

My wife hung up and I handed the phone to Colin.

"What the fuck, man?" I said. "What happened?"

"She called me and said she needed to talk with you immediately. She said it was an emergency," Colin explained, kind of apologetically, kind of in shock by the whole situation. "I told her I didn't know where you were. She told me you were at the bar with Bean, and she stayed on the phone in silence while I walked here. Is everything okay?"

Colin sat down on the stool next to me and took a breather.

"Yeah, everything is fine," I said. "Sorry to drag you into all this."

Colin looked over at Bean, and then he looked at me and said, "Let's get out of here, man."

"I'll stay for ten more minutes and then head back to the hotel, I promise."

As soon as Colin left, Bean came back over to me.

"Your friend look worried," she said. "What happen?"

"Nothing."

I wasn't in the mood to talk anymore, not even with Bean. She sat alongside me again, but I was not responding like before. She sensed that there was a problem.

"What's wrong?" she kept asking.

I didn't know what to say to her. My head was all over the place. I was worried about my marriage. I felt sorry for my wife. I thought about my lovely kids. I felt guilty, but then I tried to excuse myself by telling my conscious that I never even kissed

Bean. But of course I had every reason to feel guilty, and my wife had every reason to worry about our marriage.

I told Bean that it was time for me to go back to my hotel. I had only been in the bar a little over an hour but my bill was very high again. I was convinced that the Madasam had confused me with one of the other two falangs in the bar, but I just let it go. I had no interest in starting an argument over a relatively small sum of money. After I paid my bill, Bean walked with me to the end of Bangla Road. As we said goodbye, she took hold of both my hands and looked up at me with her beautiful soft eyes.

"You look sad, Ken," she said, sweetly. "I no want you to be alone when you sad like this."

"I am okay," I assured her. "I just need to get some sleep."

I kissed Bean on the cheek and walked back to my hotel.

The next morning I told my friends that I had a stomachache. I was in no mood to play golf. Instead, I stayed in bed until midday. It wasn't easy waiting until 4 PM for my wife's email. Of course I checked my email every five minutes to see if she sent the mail earlier, but she didn't. I wondered what kind of email she planned to send me at exactly that time. I was worried that when I opened up my email at 4 PM there would be an email from her saying, 'I want a divorce. Enjoy the rest of your trip,' or perhaps, 'Don't bother coming back. You are not welcome. Enjoy your new girl'. With these dreadful ideas whizzing around my mind, I had worked myself into quite a frenzy by the time the clock finally struck four. When I refreshed the page on my laptop screen, there was no new email, but an instant messenger box popped up on my screen.

"Ken, are you there?" my wife wrote.

"Yes, I'm here," I typed, my heart pounding from anticipation and fear. "Is everything okay?"

"Everything is okay. I will send you a link to a website now. I want you to go to the website and read the story."

My wife sent me a link to a website about Thailand. It was a forum in which thousands of people posted stories, pictures and comments about Thailand, in particular the bar scene in areas like Phuket, Pattaya and Bangkok. I opened up the link and started reading about how only a complete fool would fall in love with a bar girl. According to this story on the forum, Thai bar girls don't fall in love or develop feelings for falangs. They are just prostitutes who cheat and lie to get whatever they can from their falang customers.

"Did you read it all?" my wife asked.

"Yes. Why did you send it to me?"

"Please read this too"

My wife sent me a link to a different section of the same

website. This time the story explained how most bar girls make up a story about their parents being sick, and when the time is right they plead with the falang to give them money to pay for their parents' treatment. Dozens of comments below this article agreed that this was very common practice among bar girls throughout Thailand. Several people left comments about how they couldn't believe that some falangs were still falling for these kinds of sob stories.

I spent over an hour reading dozens of stories about Thai bar girls, and about all the ways they lie to falangs to try to get money from them. I remembered how Bean constantly talked about her sick parents and the expensive hospital fees. Even when Bean talked about her humble dream of becoming an English teacher, she managed to make me think that I could help her achieve her dream if I gave her money for English classes. And of course I remembered how my bill was suspiciously high every time I drank at Bean's bar. Yet despite all my reading, I still wasn't convinced that Bean was like the girls described on the website.

"Bean has never asked me for money," I told my wife.

"Not yet," she wrote, "but she will. Surely you can see that. All I'm asking is that you keep in mind what the website says. Enjoy your holiday with your friends and come back home the same man that I have always loved."

"Okay. I promise."

"I've gotta go now. Please don't be angry with me, and I'm sorry if I have ruined your holiday. I love you and I'm just worried that you will come back a different man."

I felt down for the rest of the day because I couldn't stop thinking about all the pain and worry that I had caused my wife. I had been so excited about coming back to Phuket that I gave little thought to how my wife must have been feeling. I went back to Bean's bar that night, only this time I wasn't the lovesick fool that I had been the previous two nights. I ordered a beer for myself and a lady drink for Bean. I didn't have to wait long before Bean started talking about her sick parents. My stomach turned. All the stuff I had read on the website earlier that day came flooding back.

"My mom need operation soon, but no money," she said.

I went along with Bean's story. I asked questions about her parents and showed concern. When she cried, I tried to comfort her with words rather than physical contact. And then the sting came.

"I ask Mamasan for 40,000 baht for mom's operation, but Mamasan say no. She say I not go with customers these days so bar not make money. But I no want to go with customers because I want be with you."

There was an awkward silence. I didn't respond because I wanted her to ask me for the money directly.

"What can I do?" she asked me. "Please tell me."

"I don't know," I said.

"Can you help me?" she asked, taking hold of my hand tenderly.

"I'm sorry. I don't have much Thai money left," I said.

"You can take it out of credit card, or ask your friend," she was quick to suggest.

"I'm sorry. I can't."

"No problem," she said, and then I noticed that she looked over at the Mamasan and shook her head ever so slightly, as if to say, 'He's not falling for it.' That horrible shake of the head showed me what was really happening. It was all a scam.

My wife was right, as usual. I was completely taken in by Bean, but fortunately my wife made me realize how foolish I had been before it was too late. I told Bean that I wasn't feeling well and had to go home early. I didn't even ask the Mamasan for the bill. I just placed the three hundred baht for the two drinks on the bar.

"Honey, what about me?" Bean asked me. "Mamasan angry with me because I only talk with you three nights. Can you give tip for me?"

"I'll give you tomorrow," I said, and then I walked away without looking back.

I never went back to Bean's bar. For the rest of the week I enjoyed golf with my mates and stayed away from Bangla Road. It felt amazing to go back home to my lovely wife and kids. I apologized to my wife sincerely. She saw how much I regretted my actions and she never held the Phuket trip against me. Thailand is a dangerous place for married men. I'm sure it has destroyed many a marriage over the years. I'm just glad it didn't destroy mine.

Premium Marriage Agency

Two months after I saw an ad for a Thai marriage agency in a Sunday newspaper, I arrived in Bangkok for the first time. As promised, the agency had a driver waiting at the arrival gates for me. He was a short, young Thai guy in a short sleeved white shirt. He grabbed my luggage and rushed me out the door towards his car. I felt very relieved that I had gotten through immigration and found the agency's driver without any problems. I had never been outside of Europe before, so I was very nervous about travelling all the way to Thailand on my own. But so far so good. Now I just had to get to my hotel and check in.

When I got into the back seat of the car, the driver handed me a goody bag complimentary of 'Thailand Premium Marriage Agency'. It contained several refreshments, a map of Bangkok, and a few Thailand souvenirs, including a fridge magnet and a keyring. The bottle of water was the only thing that interested me. I was gasping with the thirst after the long flight from England. After I finished the water, I planned to close my eyes and try to get some sleep. I was sixty-one years old, and the furthest I had ever flown was a five-hour flight from London to Turkey, so you can imagine how tired I was after the twelve hour flight to Thailand. But just as I was nodding off, the driver called my name and handed me a mobile phone.

"For you," he said.

I took the phone and said, "Hello," tentatively.

"Hello, this is Lloyd, the manager and owner of Thailand Premium Marriage Agency."

Lloyd was just giving me a quick call to welcome me to Thailand, and to see whether I would rather come into the agency today, or whether I would rather rest for the day and come in tomorrow. I thought that was great service. It certainly felt like a premium agency.

"I'd prefer to come in today and get the ball rolling," I told him.

I did manage to get some shut eye, and I only woke up when the car stopped outside a lovely four-star hotel in the middle of Bangkok. Well, I think it was the middle of Bangkok. It was a very built-up area with huge grey skyscrapers all around. The driver helped me check in. I gave him a one hundred bath tip (the smallest bill I had), and before he left he said he would be back in a couple of hours to pick me up and bring me to the agency.

The hotel room was nice but it just looked like any nice hotel in Europe. I was hoping it would have some Thai character, like silk bedclothes with a Thai design, or Thai artwork hanging on the walls, but there was nothing like that. It just looked like a clean and modern Western hotel. The only time I felt like I was in Thailand was when I turned on the TV and saw all the Thai channels. I had a quick shower to freshen up, and then I lay down on the bed for an hour to set me up for the day. I was due to meet the driver downstairs at 1 PM, but I decided to go down half an hour early and have a look around. It was a large hotel. To the right of the reception area there was a restaurant, a café, a convenience store, and a bar. There was everything I could possibly need.

I sat in the lobby and waited for the driver to arrive. There were a lot of business men and women (both Thai and foreigners) walking through the lobby, but my attention was drawn to a young

Thai woman behind the reception desk. She was there when I was checking in, but I didn't take much notice of her then. Now I had time to look at her and wonder, *Will my Thai wife be that beautiful and that young? Surely not.* I saw a Western man walk through the lobby with his Thai girlfriend. She looked no older than twenty-two, and he was in his sixties like me. It didn't look right. To be honest, I didn't want a young trophy wife. I just wanted to have a loving relationship with a genuine woman. I had been divorced twenty years already, and I was single for most of those years. God knows I tried hard to find a woman back in England, but it's hard to find love in your forties, never mind your sixties. I felt like I had already left twenty good years of my life slip by while I was waiting for someone new to come into my life. I couldn't afford to let any more years pass by like that. During our dozens of emails over the past few months, Lloyd assured me that he would be able to help me find what I was looking for.

The agency was located on the thirteenth floor of a large office building about a fifteen-minute drive from the hotel. In the agency there was one large open space in the middle that looked like the waiting area of a dental clinic. There was a lot of comfortable seating, a TV, and several glass coffee tables covered in magazines. This waiting area was surrounded by six small offices. As I followed the driver to Lloyd's office, I caught a glimpse of some of the signs on the doors. I saw 'TV room 1', 'TV room 2' and 'Recording Room'.

Lloyd was from Liverpool and he was in his late forties. He was short, but he spoke loudly and used a lot of exaggerated hand gestures, so he had a big presence. Even his clothes were flamboyant. On my first day at the agency, he was wearing a white suit with a pink tie and shirt. From the way he enunciated every word very clearly, and from his hand gestures of course, I guessed that he used to be an actor of some kind. And he was one of those guys who you would never dare ask if he was married or not, because you knew there was a good chance that he was gay. But I liked Lloyd from the start. We sat in his office for a few minutes and chatted over a coffee, and when he heard that I had not eaten since the flight, he insisted I join him for lunch.

Lloyd brought me to a cheap restaurant a couple of hundred meters down the road. The tables and chairs were plastic and there was no air conditioning, but it was clearly very popular among the locals. We were lucky to get a table.

"Are you good with chopsticks?" Lloyd asked me when we sat down.

"No, terrible."

"Alright, then I'll order fried rice for you."

Lloyd called the waitress over and ordered in Thai. I was

impressed. While we were waiting for our food, Lloyd looked around the restaurant and said, "Thai people eat out a lot. They come to this kind of cheap and cheerful restaurant for a quick lunch. The food is nothing special, but it will be good for you to have a typical Thai meal."

I was a bit apprehensive about eating Thai food for the first time, but the fried rice was nice. I mean, it was just fried rice so there wasn't much not to like.

While we were eating, Lloyd started telling me about how beautiful Thai women are and about how they make excellent wives.

"Western women have too much power these days," he said, with great conviction. "They want to wear the trousers in the house, but they also want to be treated like women. Things have gone too far. Most of them don't even look like women anymore. I can't remember the last time I saw a Western woman in a dress."

So Lloyd is not gay after all, I thought.

I didn't really agree with what Lloyd was saying, but he was speaking so passionately that I had to just nod along and let him get it off his chest.

"I have some stunning women for you," he promised. "You'll be blown away."

Then he launched into a long speech about how thousands

of stupid Western men get ripped off by bar girls every day.

"These stupid fuckin' sex tourists go to the Go-go bars and the girly bars, and they end up falling in love after a couple of days. The girl clings to the guy for the rest of his trip and bleeds him dry. When he goes back to the UK, she keeps going with customers, but the fool back in the UK keeps sending her money. How stupid can you be! Relationships with bar girls always end in tears and empty bank accounts. That's why agencies like mine are so important. We vet all the girls. We make sure they have a decent job and they have to submit a criminal background check. We only accept the best."

Lloyd paid for the meal. His agency was charging me three thousand pounds for their service, so I figured treating me to a plate of fried rice was the least he could do. On our way back to the agency, I remembered to ask Lloyd about what Thai etiquette I should be aware of.

"Avoid all public displays of affection, including holding hands. It's against their culture," he said, strongly. "Whatever you do, don't touch her head. The head is considered sacred and the cleanest part of the body. And don't point out her mistakes, like if she misunderstands something or if she uses wrong English. It will only make her lose face."

It was a lot of information to take in. It was suddenly

dawning on me that I was going to be meeting women from a completely different culture. I regretted not learning a bit more about Thai culture before I came.

Back in the agency, Lloyd brought me into 'TV Room 1' – a small office with two chairs, a desk, a small box TV and a video player.

"We still use old fashioned video tapes," Lloyd said, proudly, and then he handed me a huge catalogue. "Take your time looking through this. There's a number next to each woman. Write down the numbers of all the women who take your fancy and we will bring you their introduction videos."

"How many can I choose?" I asked.

"You can choose to watch as many videos as you like," Lloyd explained, "but you can only choose six women to meet initially."

On each page of the catalogue there were four profiles, and there were over a hundred pages. In each profile there was one picture, along with basic information like the woman's age, weight, height, occupation, interests, English skill, and whether they had children or have been married before. It was difficult to choose what to prioritize. I didn't care about their weight, age or height, but I was adamant that I didn't want to get involved with a woman with kids. The difficulty I had was deciding where to put 'English skill' on my list of priorities. At first I thought it should be priority number one, but then I saw that some of the most beautiful women in the catalogue had very little or no English. Suddenly, my priorities changed. In the end, I decided to request the videos of twenty women based purely on appearance. *I can worry about the language barrier later,* I thought.

Watching the videos, taking notes and whittling the number down to six women was a long and painful process. To be honest, after a couple of hours of looking at hundreds of profile pictures and twenty videos, it felt like there wasn't much of a difference between a lot of the women. They were all slim, pretty and much younger than me. I eventually left 'TV Room 1' with a list of six women that I wanted to meet, but when I handed the list to Lloyd, I circled the first name on the top of the list and said, "I would like to meet this girl first, please."

Her name was Som and she was the only woman that really took my breath away when I was watching the introduction videos. Som was slim and had long dark hair like the rest of the girls, but her high cheek bones and deep piercing eyes made her very striking. She was stunningly beautiful and I was desperate to meet her. Lloyd assured me that he would contact the girls straight away and arrange for me to meet all six girls over the next six days. He promised he would try to set up a date with Som first.

I was free for the rest of the afternoon while Lloyd contacted the six women on my shortlist. When I got back to the hotel, I stayed in my room because I was expecting a call from Lloyd. He eventually called with good news.

"I have lined up six dates over the next six days," he said. "As per your request, Som is first in line. Is dinner at 6 PM tomorrow evening alright?"

I was thrilled.

"That's exactly the news I was hoping for," I said. "Can you give me any tips for tomorrow?"

"Perhaps you should write down a list of questions you want to ask her," Lloyd suggested. "You will both be nervous so if there are some awkward silences, perhaps you can excuse yourself from the table and check the list of questions in the bathroom."

"Okay, good idea," I said. "How is Som's English? Her profile said her English skill is low."

"You'll be able to have a basic conversation with her. Or, if you prefer, an interpreter can join you for dinner."

"No, that won't be necessary. That would be too awkward."

As soon as I finished the call with Lloyd, I grabbed a pen of paper and headed downstairs to the café. With a cup of coffee, I sat back and wracked my brain for a couple of dozen questions I could ask Som if we found ourselves struggling for something to talk about. I kept the questions light, like 'Have you travelled much?', 'How did you learn English?' and so on. They were very basic questions, but I was worried that I would be so nervous that I might not be able to think of anything to say. When I finished the list, I folded up the paper and placed it in my wallet for safe-keeping.

That night the agency put on a walking tour for its clients because they knew we were at a loose end at night. Half a dozen of us met a Thai tour guide in the lobby of the hotel at 7 PM. There were several Western men from the agency staying in the hotel. First we went for a meal near the hotel and then we jumped into two taxis and headed to the Chao Phraya river. The river was beautiful at night. Across the river I could see modern sky scrapers towering above the city, but to my left there was a beautiful old Buddhist temple lit up by soft yellow lighting. It was a stunning view. As we walked, we talked about our experiences in Thailand so far. All the other guys had been in Bangkok for at least four days, so they had already started meeting women. They all said how beautiful and kind the women were, and they spoke very highly of Lloyd and the great service he was providing.

After our stroll along the river, the guide brought us to a huge night market for some shopping. I wasn't interested in buying anything, but the other guys in the group bought bags and bags of counterfeit T-shirts, wallets, sunglasses and cologne. I was hoping to spend only half an hour in the market, but haggling with the market vendors took ages – every small purchase took about ten minutes. I was stuck following the group around the market for almost two hours. When we finally got back to our hotel, I had a few beers from the mini-bar and I conked out around midnight.

I must have been exhausted from the long journey and the walking tour, because the next day I didn't wake up until noon. But once I woke up, I felt really positive about my first full day in Thailand. I was looking forward to meeting Som. I had some time to kill before our date, so I ate breakfast downstairs and read a book in the café. It was a lovely relaxing afternoon. Before I knew it, it was time to get ready for my date. I threw on my smartest blue shirt and trousers, and then I headed downstairs to meet the agency driver. He drove me to a large, quiet restaurant about twenty minutes from the hotel. Som was already waiting for me inside. She stood up as I approached, and then she placed her two hands together and gave me a Thai-style bow. Som looked even more beautiful in person. She was wearing a cute black and white pok-a-dot dress, and her hair was much wavier than in her introduction video. We sat down and tried to talk to each other. I could tell straight away that her English was not very good. I quickly realized that I had to make my sentences very short and very simple to have any chance of making her understand what I was saying. Even though we struggled with a language barrier from the start, we bonded immediately. There was a special chemistry between us. I had a list of questions in my wallet for emergencies, but I didn't need it. Som was quite talkative and I felt completely at ease around her, so I was able to talk freely.

I already knew from her profile that Som was twenty six years old and that she worked as a receptionist in a small import/export company, but over dinner I learned that Som's dream was to get married to a nice man and have children. She said she loved Thailand, but she was willing to live in another country if she found a good foreign man. All this was music to my ears. I had heard loads of stories about guys meeting Thai women through marriage agencies and proposing to them after only a few days or even a few hours. Those stories always sounded crazy to me, but now I could kind of understand what those guys were thinking. I had this amazing connection with this beautiful, warm Thai woman, and I was afraid that if I didn't snap her up quickly, she might disappear from my life.

There was a large pond full of a couple of dozen carp at the side of the restaurant. I brought Som there and we sat together on one of the benches. She seemed to take great delight in looking at the carp. She looked like such a pure and innocent young woman. While she looked at the fish, I looked at Som and thought, *I'd like nothing more than to take you back to England and make you my wife.* Overcome with feelings for Som, I reached over and tried to take hold of her hand gently. She pulled her hand away in surprise and giggled awkwardly. I felt terrible for moving too fast. I apologized to Som repeatedly. I could see that she was a good Thai woman and I didn't want to disrespect her or her culture.

When we were leaving the restaurant, Som said, "I hope see you again sometime."

"Of course we will," I said. "How about tomorrow?"

"But I think Lloyd introduce you new girl tomorrow and new girl next day and next day."

"I don't want to meet other girl," I said, sincerely. "I only want to meet you. Would you like to meet me tomorrow?"

Som agreed to meet me again the next day. I asked the driver to bring me to the agency so that I could speak with Lloyd urgently. Lloyd burst out laughing when I told him to cancel the other five dates.

"Why?" he asked. "The dates are already arranged. Why not just meet them and see what happens?"

"No," I said, emphatically. "It's wrong. I have something special with Som. I don't think it would be right to see other girls.

I'm here for three weeks, so I'll let things play out with Som first. If things don't work out for some reason, then I can meet another girl, one at a time."

Lloyd thought I was being silly, but he went ahead and cancelled the dates with the five other girls. I asked one more favor of Lloyd. I told him how much I liked the riverside view on my first night in Bangkok, so I asked him to set up my second date with Som in a romantic riverside restaurant.

Lloyd came through for me. I met Som the following day in a restaurant with a stunning river view. It was the perfect setting for a romantic meal. Som was as lovely and as charming as she was on the first date. After the meal, we walked along the river, and I got an amazing thrill when Som let me hold her hand. The three thousand pounds I had paid to Lloyd's agency was worth it. I had found my future wife – no doubt about it. It was sad to say goodbye to Som again, but we made a plan to meet the next evening for dinner. She was working during the day, and she slept early at night, so on weekdays we could only meet in the evenings.

When I got back to my room, I got a call from Lloyd asking me if I wanted to join his other clients on a tour to a rooftop bar and another night market. I told him that I was exhausted and just wanted to rest in my hotel. But that wasn't exactly true. The truth was that I had no interest in walking around another night market for two hours. I just wanted to relax in my room and have a few beers from the mini-bar.

At around 11 PM I was on my fourth beer and feeling tipsy. I didn't want to be stuck in my hotel room alone anymore. I decided to head down to the hotel bar on the first floor. As I expected, the bar was not busy. Most of the tables were empty and there was only one guy sitting at the bar. I also sat at the bar and ordered a Jack and coke. The other guy at the bar was a fellow English lad called Frank. He was in his early thirties, and he was a little drunk so he was eager to talk. At first Frank talked about himself a lot. He told me in great detail about his job in IT, but I am computer illiterate so I had no idea what he was talking about. He regularly came to Thailand on business trips, and as a result he could speak Thai quite well. Frank was fascinated to hear that I had come to Thailand with the sole purpose of meeting a Thai woman through a marriage agency.

"I didn't know that kind of thing still goes on," he said, surprised.

Frank went on to bombard me with question after question about the agency, the women, the process, the fee and so on. His fascination soon turned into cynicism. He thought three thousand pound was a lot of money to pay just to be introduced to women.

I explained that all the women are vetted and only the best are accepted by the agency, but Frank just shook his head and said, "Three thousand pound! Jesus!"

When Frank asked me about my time in Thailand so far, he was surprised to hear how limited my experiences had been.

"Have you even been to Siam Square? he asked.

"What's that?"

"Jesus! It's the huge shopping area near here. It's just down the road, maybe a ten-minute walk at most."

"I haven't walked around this area," I said. "I've only left the hotel with the agency driver or tour guide."

"Have you at least been to Sukhumvit?" Frank laughed.

"Is that a place?"

"Jesus! You've never heard of Sukhumvit or Nana or Soi Cowboy?"

"Never," I said, a little embarrassed of my ignorance.

"You can't come to Bangkok and not visit Sukhumvit. I'm going there after this drink. Come with me."

"It's late. It's almost midnight."

"Exactly. That's the best time to go."

Frank explained that Sukhumvit was a tourist area with hundreds of hotels, bars, restaurants, massage parlors and a lot of Go-go bars and other kinds of girly bars. It all sounded too loud and wild for me. I told Frank to go without me. He finished his drink quickly and left.

As soon as Frank left, I started to reflect on some of the things we had talked about. Frank laughed at me for not knowing anything about Bangkok, but then again he was right to laugh. I came all the way to Thailand and I let myself be stuck in a small bubble that the agency had created. It was pathetic. Perhaps it was the alcohol that gave me the courage to suddenly want to step out of the bubble and experience more of Bangkok. I paid my bill and rushed out of the bar to catch up with Frank. Fortunately, I found him in the lobby waiting for a taxi.

The taxi dropped us off at the entrance of Nana Plaza. I was gobsmacked as soon as I stepped out of the taxi. First of all, I was shocked by the huge crowds of people on the street and in the bars. The place was hectic. I was also taken aback by how many ladyboys there were hanging around the entrance of Nana Plaza. I had never seen a ladyboy before, and now they seemed to be everywhere. Before I came to Thailand, I had heard that Thai ladyboys are very beautiful and often pass as real women, but not the ladyboys outside of Nana. They were all over six feet tall and they were wearing high heels so they towered above everybody. They also had huge breasts and fat lips. Another thing that surprised me was the amount of Western men walking around.

They were everywhere. I had no idea there were so many foreigners in Bangkok.

I followed Frank into Nana Plaza. First, we had a beer at one of the bars in the open area on the ground floor.

"Let's have a quick beer here to let you acclimatize. Then we can go upstairs to one of the Go-go bars."

"Frank, you know, I kind of have a girlfriend now," I said. "I don't think I should go to a Go-go bar."

"Nonsense," he said. "You can go and look, but just don't touch any of the girls."

I had come all this way to Thailand and I thought it only fair that I go into a Thai Go-go bar once for the experience. Som would never find out.

When Frank brought me upstairs, we passed a ladyboy bar. There were a dozen ladyboys in bikinis standing outside the bar trying to get customers to go inside. Surprisingly, several of them greeted Frank and they knew him by name. He noticed the surprise on my face.

"I admit it," he said. "Sometimes I'm in the mood for something different, so I go with a ladyboy. Shoot me."

"Not at all," I said. "Each to their own."

Frank brought me into a Go-go bar on the second floor. We were welcomed warmly and the waitress led us to two seats right in front of the stage. There were five girls dancing in bright yellow bikinis. Frank ordered two beers while I stared at the girls with wide eyes. I had never been to this kind of bar before. I had never even been to a strip joint back in England.

"What do you think?" Frank asked.

"It's amazing," I said. "They're all beautiful."

All five of the dancers were in their twenties and they were stunning.

"What happens in this kind of bar?" I asked Frank.

"If you like a girl, you can pay the bar a barfine, take the girl to a short time room for an hour and pay her for her services. Is there a girl you like already?"

"I like them all," I said, giggling with excitement and nervous energy, "but I'm only gonna look. I wouldn't cheat on my girlfriend."

After about five minutes, the music stopped suddenly and the five girls left the stage.

"What's happening?" I asked Frank.

"They rotate the dancers. Five new girls will come on stage in a second."

A few minutes later, five new girls appeared. The music came on again and the girls started dancing. Suddenly, one of the girls stopped dancing and was frozen in one spot on the stage. I hadn't looked at the new girls closely, but when this girl stopped suddenly, I looked at her and I was heartbroken to see it was Som. We stared at each other in shock for a second, and then she ran off the stage.

"What just happened?" Frank asked me. "Why did that girl stare at you like that and then run off?"

I couldn't respond to Frank. I was in shock. I was shaking. My breath became quick and short. Frank was worried that I would hyper ventilate, so he patted my shoulder gently and told me to take deep breaths and calm down. I put my face in my hands and shook my head in disbelief.

"What the fuck did I just see?" I said out loud.

"That's what I want to know," Frank said.

"I need to get out of here. Can you pay the bill and I'll meet you downstairs?"

Frank brought me to the quietest bar he could find on Soi 4. I told him that the dancer who ran off the stage was the girl I had met through the agency.

"You paid three thousand pounds to an agency to meet a Go-go girl," Frank concluded. "That's a joke!"

I woke up early the next morning and got a taxi to Thailand Premium Marriage Agency. I was livid. I told Lloyd that

Som was a Go-go dancer, and I demanded a full refund.

"I can't give you a refund just because of one girl," he said. "We have hundreds of other girls. Choose another one."

"How can I trust your agency to introduce me to a nice girl now? I mean, I thought you said you vet the girls and only accept the best."

"We do. We do.," Lloyd insisted, desperate to protect his agency's reputation. "I don't know what happened. Some Thai girls are very cunning. She obviously lied to us too."

Eventually, Lloyd agreed to give me half my money back. But it wasn't even about the money. The problem was that I had developed genuine feelings for Som, and I had allowed myself to imagine a bright future with this beautiful Thai woman. It was devastating to find out that all my feelings for Som and all my hopes for the future with her had been built on lies. I brought my flight forward by a couple of weeks. I just wanted to go back to the comfort of my own home and get back into a routine. I wanted to forget all about Thai women and marriage agencies. Back here in England, alone, the years keep slipping by.

Caught on Camera

Noah was walking along Beach Road with his mate, Andy, on their second evening in Pattaya, and Andy was trying to get him to go for a massage. Andy had the same routine every time he came to Thailand - massage in the early evening, then dinner, then drinks and a bar girl at the end of the night.

"No massage for me," Noah insisted. "Not after last night."

"We can go to a legit massage store this time. Nobody will try to have sex with you or give you a happy ending."

"I don't think there are any legit massage places in Pattaya, mate."

"Of course there are, up on Second Road."

Noah hesitated for a moment. He had a girlfriend, Denise, back home. He had to be careful.

"Are you sure they are legit?" Noah asked. "I don't want

another shit massage from a prostitute."

"Yes, they are legit. They're all licensed and everything."

Noah had to trust his friend when it came to all things Pattaya. Whereas Noah had only visited Pattaya once before, Andy had been coming twice a year for the past twelve years, since he was eighteen. So, they made the short walk up to Second Road to get a no-extras-offered massage. The first massage shop Andy brought Noah to had six beautiful Thai women sitting outside.

"Not here," Noah said. "There's no way this place is legit."

Andy sighed deeply at his friend's stubbornness.

"Okay. Let's walk a bit more."

A hundred meters further down Second Road, Noah and Andy stopped outside a large, modern looking massage parlor.

"Is this place okay?" Andy asked.

Noah looked through the glass door. There were four attractive female masseuses sitting around a coffee table. They looked very professional in their beige uniforms.

"Okay. Let's give it a go."

Both Noah and Andy chose a body massage. They were brought towards the back of the salon where there was a row of four small private areas curtained off by heavy blue cloth that reached from the ceiling to the floor. Noah was led into the first curtained off area by one of the beautiful young women.

"Take off clothes to your underpants and lay down on stomach," she said, very softly. "I come back two minutes."

Five minutes later the masseuse returned. She introduced herself as Bee. First, Bee massaged Noah's shoulders and neck. She started talking to Noah when she moved on to his back. She asked him all the usual questions:

"Where you from?"

"England."

"How long you stay Pattaya?"

"We arrived yesterday morning. We will fly to Phuket in three days."

"This first time in Thailand?"

"No, it's my second time."

Bee moved onto the legs, but Noah noticed that she was rushing the massage a bit. That wasn't a good sign.

"Turn over please."

Noah was proud of himself for not having an erection when he turned onto his back. He looked at Bee's eyes closely to see if she would check out his crotch area. She didn't. Now that Noah was on his back, he couldn't help but look at Bee and notice that she was a very beautiful woman. She had long, straight black hair, fare skin and narrow features. Noah felt blood surging into his penis. He had a semi. This was dangerous. He closed his eyes and forced himself to think about what he would eat for dinner and what presents he could buy for people back home. It worked. His semi went away and he was able to open his eyes again. Bee had one oily hand on each thigh. She rubbed down to Noah's knees and then moved her hands up slowly. Noah noticed that her fingers were going further and further up, to the point where the tip of her fingers were going beneath his underpants. After a few more slow rubs, her hands were all the way under his underpants, and the tips of her fingers were getting close to his testicles. Now he was fully erect. When Bee's fingers finally reached Noah's testicles, she bypassed them and went straight for his penis. With her soft oily hand, she gave Noah's penis one slow stroke and whispered, "You want boom boom?"

Noah was extremely turned on. He wanted nothing more than to have 'boom boom' with Bee, but he couldn't do that to his girlfriend back home.

"No, sorry," Noah whispered. "I can't."

"Okay. No problem," Bee smiled. "I massage more."

Bee continued the massage below the knees, but Noah stopped her.

"It's okay. Let's just finish," he said, as gently as he could. "I have to go."

Bee looked surprised and a little embarrassed. She

gathered her oils and her extra towels, and she disappeared through the blue curtain. When Noah got dressed, he said in a raised voice, "I'm done. I'll wait for you in the McDonalds down the road."

Through one of the curtains, and a little out of breath, Andy responded, "Right, see ya later."

Noah sipped on a milkshake while he waited for his friend. He wondered whether Andy had known that the masseuse would offer sex at the end of the massage. *Of course he knew,* Noah concluded. *That fucker knows Pattaya inside out.* Before Noah could finish his milkshake, Andy came bursting through the front entrance of McDonalds and scanned the room frantically in search of his friend. He was in a panic about something. He rushed over to Noah and said, "Let's get out of here. I think the girl from last night spotted me."

Noah wanted to clear away his milkshake, but Andy took it out of his hand and slammed it on the table.

"There's no time for that," he said, as he started pushing his friend out the door.

When they got outside, Noah turned around and asked, "What's the problem? Who cares if she saw you?"

"She's really clingy. If she sees me, I won't be able to get rid of her for the rest of the night."

Andy was looking down the road to see if the clingy woman was following him. "Let's move!"

He started running down the road and Noah had to follow him. After about a hundred meters, Andy came to a sudden stop outside a restaurant.

"Let's get dinner in here," he said. "I've been here before. It's nice."

They sat all the way in the back so that the woman from last night would not see them if she passed by.

When they sat down at the table, Noah started laughing at his friend because he was freaking out over a girl.

"Thank Christ!" Andy let out a sigh of relief, as he wiped the sweat from his brow.

"Is she really that bad?" Noah asked.

"She's a nightmare! I had to threaten to call the hotel's reception just to get her out of my room this morning."

Andy ordered a beer with his dinner, while Noah got a coke.

"Get a beer, for fuck sake!"

Noah lifted up his phone and showed his friend the time – 8:20 PM.

"Okay. Okay," Andy nodded his head. "Not before 10 PM, I know."

Andy made two special rules for this trip: He would not touch a drop of alcohol before ten o' clock, and he was only allowed six beers a night. He made these rules to avoid getting drunk. There was a lot of temptation in Thailand, especially in Pattaya, so he was afraid that if he got drunk, he would end up doing something he might regret.

Noah and Andy got their food and ate it quickly. Within half an hour of entering the restaurant, they were ready to leave.

"There's a bar I know near here. Let's go for a few drinks there to start the night off," Andy suggested.

"I'll go to the bar, but I'm not drinking before ten o' clock."

"It's almost nine. You can start an hour early, can't ya?"

"No. Not a minute before ten o' clock," Noah said, much to his friend's frustration.

Andy didn't mind having a beer on his own over dinner, but he hated the idea of going to a bar and being the only one drinking, even if it was for just an hour. They had to make a new plan. They ended up sitting in the restaurant with empty plates in front of them until half nine, and then they decided to make their way slowly towards Soi Buakhao.

Noah followed his friend to a large complex with dozens of small girly bars under the same roof. They all had square bars with stools along each side. There were half a dozen or more girls behind each bar, and all the bars had two poles in the center for the girls to dance around. Andy led Noah to a bar in the center of the complex. Three of the girls came over to Andy and welcomed him warmly.

"Long time no see," one of them said. "Andy, when you arrive Pattaya?"

"Today," he lied.

In the past few days, Noah saw dozens of girls come up to Andy and call him by his name. He was well known around town.

It was busy, but Noah and Andy were lucky to find two empty stools at the bar. They sat down and ordered two beers. Noah looked at his phone – 10:01 PM. He could start drinking. Noah drank his beer slowly and kept to himself, while Andy was enjoying being the center of attention. He was a larger-than-life character and all the girls seemed to love him. He drank his beer quickly and rang the bell. A big cheer erupted because it meant that everyone would get a free drink on Andy. All the girls bowed to him to show their appreciation.

"That's gonna cost you a fortune," Noah commented.

"Fuck it. I love this bar," Andy shouted into his friend's ear.

"You've been with one of the girls?"

"Mate, I've been with all of them," Andy said proudly, "and some of them more than once."

As the night went on, two girls sat with Andy and took up all of his attention, leaving Noah alone with his beer. He ended up chatting with one of the girls behind the bar called Kwan. Noah was drawn to Kwan because she looked like a Thai version of the girl next door. Her hair was straight and simple, her clothes were plain and she didn't seem to wear any make up. Yet she was very beautiful. Noah bought her a drink, and Kwan came out from behind the bar to sit on the stool next to him. Their conversation was often awkward and full of silences because Kwan's English wasn't great, but Noah felt comfortable sitting with her. After midnight, Noah was starting to feel tipsy. The conversation with Kwan was flowing much better now and they were flirting more – subtle touches of the lower back, prolonged eye contact and eventually they were holding hands. Noah let it go this far because he knew that he could stop at any moment. Andy was pleased to see that his friend was finally giving into temptation. He leant over to Kwan and asked her, "If I ring the bell again, will you kiss my friend?"

"Sure," she replied happily. "Why not?"

Noah looked happy too. Andy rang the bell and another cheer went up. Noah and Kwan held each other gently by the waist and leant in for a kiss. They ended up making out for five minutes. After that, Kwan excused herself and went to the bathroom.

Andy turned to Noah and said, "Mate, you know you have to barfine her, right?"

Noah looked like he was dangling over the edge of temptation with one hand.

"I don't know," he said, shaking his head, looking tortured.

"You've been sitting with her for over an hour, you've kissed her. You have to barfine her, otherwise you've just wasted her time."

"Ah, don't say that."

"Mate, just go for it. Kwan is good, trust me. You won't regret it."

"But I will regret it. That's the point."

Noah started his sixth and final beer. He knew he had to make a decision about Kwan soon. She was beautiful and sweet, and they had a special chemistry. His girlfriend was thousands of miles away. She would never find out. It would make no difference to her if he slept with Kwan or not. Noah started off by making this argument in his head, but in the end he knew that he couldn't go through with it. He planned to marry Denise, and he didn't want to live with the guilt for the rest of his life. Noah held Kwan by the hand and told her gently that he wouldn't be able to barfine her. He didn't mention his girlfriend; he just said that he wanted to be alone. Kwan gave Noah sad puppy eyes, but he knew that she would move on to another falang as soon as he was out of sight. Nonetheless, he handed her five hundred baht because he felt terrible for sitting with her for most of the night when she could have been using that time trying to find a genuine customer. Noah finished his last beer and went back to his hotel alone, leaving Andy in the bar to enjoy the rest of the night.

The next morning Noah was awoken by loud and frantic banging on the door.

"Open up," Andy yelled.

"What time is it?" Noah asked when he opened door.

"It's eight o' clock. I haven't been to sleep yet. The two girls just left," Andy replied, stepping into the room quickly and closing the door behind him. He looked flustered.

"Why the fuck did you wake me up so early?"

"I've got something to show you," Andy said, sounding very serious. "You'll need to sit down for this."

They both sat down at the edge of the bed. Andy held out his phone and pressed play on a Youtube video. Noah watched the video closely, while Andy kept his eyes on his friend to see his reaction. Noah's jaw dropped as soon as the video started.

"Is that the bar we were in last night?"

"Yep."

With his eyes glued to the screen, and with a voice full of disgust, Andy asked, "Who took this video?"

"Some Youtuber. He was doing a live stream. He must have been sitting in the bar next to ours, but you can obviously see us in the background."

The video was almost three hours long, and Noah and Andy were in almost all of it. Andy forwarded the video to the part where Noah and Kwan kissed.

Noah jumped to his feet suddenly and screamed, "Fuck!"

He started to pace up and down the room in a panic.

"How did you find this?" he asked Andy.

"A mate back home sent it to me."

"Is that Youtuber famous?"

"Kinda. He's one of the most popular falang Youtubers in Thailand."

"Oh fuck! What if Denise sees it?"

"She probably won't."

"But she might. Someone might show it to her. How can he go around videoing people like that?"

"It's fucked up, especially in Pattaya. Anyway, mate, I need some sleep," Andy said, as he stood up and put his hand on his friend's shoulder. "Don't worry about it. Denise will never see the video anyway."

Noah was outraged that someone had recorded him secretly and put it up on Youtube for all the world to see. After Andy went back to his room, Noah turned on his laptop to watch the video again. Then he started watching other videos from this Youtuber. His name was Pat, and his Youtube channel was called 'Pat Thai'. He had videos of several Asian countries, but most of his videos were of Thailand. Noah found the videos really boring. In almost all of the videos, Pat was just walking in a tourist area in Bangkok or Pattaya at night, recording all the people passing by and the working girls looking for customers. He commented on the things he saw and gave information about bars, hotels, food and prices as he walked the streets. He also did marathon live streams at night that sometimes lasted up to eight hours. If he was having a beer in a bar, he would often place his phone on the table facing out so that it would record all the street action and not him. Noah was disgusted by this because those people walking by or sitting in the bar across the street had no idea they were being broadcasted on Youtube. Pat rarely showed his face, but on some of the live streams he did speak into the camera. He was a skinny, geeky looking guy from America in his late thirties.

"How the fuck is this guy popular?" Noah asked, aloud.

Noah spent a full hour looking through dozens of videos, and then he got excited when he saw that Pat was due to start a new live stream in ten minutes. Noah sat on the edge of his bed waiting impatiently for it to start. He hoped that Pat would be streaming from somewhere easily recognizable, like Walking Street or Beach Road so that he could go and ask him in person to take down his live stream from last night. But, unfortunately for Noah, Pat started his live stream from a massage parlor. He was getting a foot massage, and of course the camera was pointing at the female masseuse. Noah didn't recognize the massage parlor or the woman, but he knew a man who might. He picked up his laptop and ran next door. It took several minutes of banging on the door before Andy finally opened it.

"What the fuck! I just fell asleep," Andy said, irritated and still a little drunk.

"Look at this. He just started a new live stream."

"What about it?"

"Where is it?"

"How the fuck should I know?"

"I thought you knew every massage place in Pattaya."

"Well I don't know that one. I'm goin' back to bed."

"No, come on. I need your help. When he finishes the massage, he'll go outside and I need you to tell me where he is."

"For what?"

"So that we can go and tell him to take down the fuckin'

video."

Andy started laughing at his friend's ludicrous idea.

"Are ya serious?" he asked. "Your gonna track him down, are ya?"

"Yes. I don't want Denise seeing that video."

"Why the fuck would Denise watch an old live stream from Thailand?"

"Someone might show it to her. Come on, you gotta help me."

Andy closed his eyes and leant his head against the door. He was exhausted, but he couldn't refuse his friend in an hour of need. With his eyes still closed, he replied, "Okay, I'll help you, but let me run to the 7eleven around the corner first. I need a beer. Hair of the dog an' all."

"Good idea. Get me a few too."

"But it's not 10 PM. It's not even 10 AM. What happened to your precious rule?" Andy teased.

"I don't care. I need a drink."

Noah and Andy watched Pat Thai's live stream with a few cool morning beers. The foot massage lasted half an hour. When Pat was leaving the massage parlor, Andy and Noah sat closely to the screen to get a good look at what street he was stepping out onto. But when Pat stepped outside, for some reason he pointed the camera down at the ground while he was walking. He walked for only a short minute and then popped into a 7eleven.

Noah turned to Andy and asked, "Do you recognize that 7eleven?"

"Do I heck! They all look the same."

Pat spent the next ten minutes talking about the selection of soft drinks on offer.

"Do people really watch this shit?" Noah asked.

"Over three hundred people are watching it now," Andy replied.

When Pat finally came out of 7eleven, he held his camera at eye level and filmed the people and stores he passed. Andy looked closely.

"Well, do you know what street he's on?" Noah asked impatiently.

Andy saw something on the street that made everything click.

"He's on Soi 13," he said excitedly. "He's heading to Beach Road."

They both put down their beers and hurried out the door. Andy was happy just to walk quickly, but as soon as they left the hotel, Noah started sprinting and Andy had to keep pace. Their hotel was on Soi 10, so they didn't have far to go. When they reached Beach Road, Noah turned on Youtube on his phone, but Pat's live stream was already finished.

"What do we do now?" Noah asked, panicking. "Which way?"

"He's probably heading towards Walking Street," Noah suggested.

They started running towards Walking Street, and just as they passed Soi Post Office, Pat came into view twenty meters up ahead. He was walking slowly along Beach Road, but then he stopped to talk with a taxi driver who was parked at the side of the road.

"Hurry, before he gets in the taxi," Noah urged his friend to run again.

Pat was about to get into the back of the taxi when Noah called out, "Wait! Wait one minute, please!"

Pat turned around and was surprised to see two falangs running towards him.

"Everything okay?" he asked.

"You're Pat Thai, right?" Noah asked.

"Yes."

"Look, I know you didn't mean to, but on your live stream last night you filmed us drinking in a girly bar on Soi Buakhao."

"Oh, I see," Pat laughed awkwardly. "So, what can I do?"

"Well, in the video I am making out with one of the bar girls."

"We need you to delete the video from Youtube," Andy stepped forward and tried to be intimidating.

"Guys, I'm sorry, but I'm a content creator. I'm not going to delete my contents just because you were kissing a girl in the background."

At this point, the taxi driver got out of the taxi and said to Pat, "We go now."

"Guys, I've got to go," Pat said. "Sorry I can't help you."

Noah grabbed Pat by the arm to stop him getting into the taxi.

"You don't understand. I have a girlfriend back home," he explained, a little desperately. "If she sees that video, I'm fucked. Please delete it."

"I'm sorry about that, but this is my job," Pat looked intimidated, but he was standing his ground.

"You shouldn't be videoing people secretly anyway," Andy said, with a noticeably raised voice.

"It's perfectly legal to film in public places," Pat responded without hesitation, and it sounded like he had defended himself with that exact sentence dozens of times before.

"Mate, don't be a prick!" Andy said.

The taxi driver was getting more annoyed as he watched the three falangs argue about something he could not understand. He started yelling at them in Thai. Pat wanted to wrap things up quickly. He turned to Noah and said with a smug look on his face, "If you have a girlfriend back home, perhaps you shouldn't be making out with bar girls in Pattaya. Now, if you don't mind, I really have to go."

Pat tried to get into the back of the taxi, but Noah grabbed him by the arm again (this time more aggressively) and pulled him back. Pat fell to the ground.

"You're going nowhere until you delete the video," Noah shouted down at him.

The taxi driver ran around the car and jumped in between Noah and Pat. Rather than acting as a peace maker, he was the angriest of them all. He started yelling in Thai right in Noah's face. Noah tried to push the taxi driver aside so that he could get to Pat. The situation had escalated quickly and Andy was worried it was going to get worse. After years of coming to Thailand, he knew that this kind of situation never ended well for falangs. Andy grabbed hold of his friend and tried to speak some sense into him.

"You know what's happening here, don't ya?" he said calmly. "We are getting in the way of the taxi driver making a fare. That's why he's angry. You're costing him money. You have to let him go. If the police get involved, they always side with Thai locals. Always."

"When that prick deletes the video, they can go."

"Mate, drop it for now or shit will really hit the fan."

Reluctantly, Noah had to step back and allow Pat to get into the taxi.

"Just delete the fucking video!" he shouted before the door closed and the taxi drove off.

Andy brought Noah to a nearby restaurant to get something for breakfast. While they were waiting for their food, Noah kept his eye on Youtube. He jolted upright in his chair when he saw that Pat Thai had started a new live stream from the back of the taxi.

"What's he saying?" Andy asked.

"He's on his way to Bangkok," Noah replied, deep in thought.

"Good riddance. You can send him a message on Youtube later and ask him again to delete the video."

"You heard him. He's a content creator and he won't delete his content. What a prick! We need to go to Bangkok and talk to him again."

"Oh God!" Andy sighed, slumping back in his chair. "Drop it

already!"

"What if Denise sees it? I don't want this video hanging over me for the rest of my life."

"Even if we go to Bangkok and track him down, what will you do? You said yourself that he won't delete it."

"We'll corner him and make him delete it."

"Mate, you go, and I'll stay here."

"And do what?"

"Sleep. I'm wrecked."

"You can sleep in the taxi on the way there and on the way back. It won't take long."

"But what makes you so sure you'll be able to find him?"

"I've seen his videos of Bangkok. He always goes to the Sukhumvit area. We can just watch his live stream and track him down that way, like we did earlier."

Andy rubbed his eyes furiously in frustration. This was not how he wanted to spend his holiday.

"Was it worth it?" Andy asked.

"What?"

"The kiss, was it worth it? You could have at least fucked her."

Andy fell fast asleep in the taxi while Noah watched Youtube. It takes about an hour and a half from Pattaya to

Sukhumvit by taxi, and Pat Thai kept his live stream going the whole time, talking about how sick he was of Pattaya and how he needed a change of scenery. But unfortunately for Noah, Pat Thai mentioned that he was approaching Sukhumvit and had to stop the live stream while he looked for a hotel. Andy woke up when they got off the highway in Bangkok, and the first thing he asked was, "Where is your friend now?"

"Don't know," Noah answered. "He stopped his live stream."

"Great! So what do we do now?"

"We hang around Sukhumvit until he starts his live stream again. I'm sure it won't be long."

They got off at Nana Station and went for a coffee while they waited. An hour later Pat Thai started a new live stream, but Noah was disappointed to see that he was live streaming from his hotel room.

"Do you recognize the room?" Noah asked Andy, clasping at straws.

"No, of course not."

They couldn't believe their ears when Pat Thai said this was only a quick live stream to let people know that he planned to sleep for the rest of the day, but he promised to live stream again that night.

"What a waste of time!" Andy sighed. "Let's go back to Pattaya."

"No, come on, we have to wait," Noah insisted, unable to give up.

"Wait all day? Mate, don't let it ruin your holiday. More importantly, don't let it ruin mine. Let's go back to Pattaya and enjoy ourselves. Just send him a fuckin' message online."

Noah didn't reply. He was annoyed that his friend didn't appreciate the difficult situation he was in. They sat in silence in front of empty coffee cups for almost half an hour. Eventually Andy gave in and said, "If you really insist on waiting all day, then we should at least check into a cheap hotel and get some sleep. I'm exhausted."

"Agreed."

"Paid by you, of course."

"Of course."

Andy knew Sukhumvit well, so they had no problem finding a twin room in a cheap hotel. As soon as they checked in, Andy climbed into bed and fell asleep almost instantly. Noah was too anxious to sleep, but he tried to take his mind off of his problems by watching TV shows on his phone, and he constantly checked Youtube just in case Pat Thai started live streaming earlier than planned. Andy slept right through the afternoon to the late evening, and when he woke up they went for dinner in a pizza joint. There was still no sign of Pat Thai.

Over dinner, Andy asked, "Mate, how long are you gonna follow that guy?"

Noah looked his friend in the eyes and said slowly, "As long as it takes."

"I'm willing to stay in Bangkok tonight, but remember that we have an early flight to Phuket booked for the day after tomorrow, so we have to go back to Pattaya tomorrow."

Noah didn't respond.

"I am not missing that flight," Andy added.

After dinner, somewhat predictably, Andy suggested going for a massage.

"I'm not in the mood," Noah said. "You go. I'll wait in McDonalds again."

Andy decided to skip his evening massage for one day, and instead the two friends walked around Sukhumvit for a while, half hoping to bump into Pat Thai, or at least hoping that he would start his live stream soon. As 10 PM approached, Andy insisted that they head to Soi 4 and start drinking. Noah was in no mood for drinking or crowded bars, but he felt obliged to go because Andy had given up a night in Pattaya to come help him in Bangkok.

First, they went for a quick drink in a surprisingly quiet Irish bar called Fitzgeralds on Soi 4, and then they moved onto the always-crowded Stumble Inn next to the entrance of Nana Plaza. Andy was determined to get drunk quickly, going through three beers in an hour with ease. In contrast, Noah wanted to keep his wits about him, so he nursed his second beer for over an hour. Stumble Inn was packed and there were beautiful Thai woman (mostly freelancers) everywhere. Andy walked around the bar talking to dozens of women until he eventually clicked with one beautiful young woman named Aom. They got on so well that Andy decided to take her to one of the short time rooms in Nana Plaza.

"Are you okay here on your own?" he asked Noah, as Aom dragged him out of the bar.

"Yes, go on," Noah replied. "Call me when you're done."

Noah went to wait in McDonalds at the top of Soi 4. He ordered a Big Mac meal and sat by the side window. It was a great seat because he could watch all the freelancers – both ladies and ladyboys – walk around to the outside toilets at the back. It was now after midnight, but finally, after a twelve hour wait, Pat Thai started live streaming again. Noah dropped his burger and grabbed his phone excitedly with both hands. He was glad to see that Pat Thai was not in his hotel room this time; he was in a busy bar with a lot of falangs in the background. But Noah didn't recognize the bar. He tried to give Andy a call but it rang out. Noah sent him a message telling him to turn on Pat Thai's live stream to see if he recognized the bar. Noah didn't hold out much hope of getting a reply. He kept looking at the live stream carefully, and it soon became clear that Pat Thai was very drunk. He was slurring his words and the camera was moving all over the place. Then he announced that he was leaving the bar to go get something to eat. Noah sensed his chance was coming. He pulled the phone closer to his face as Pat Thai stepped out of the bar and onto a ridiculously crowded and noisy street. He recognized the street immediately.

"Kao San Road!" Noah blurted out loudly.

Noah rushed out the door and jumped in a taxi.

Noah kept watching the live stream from the back of the taxi. He watched closely as Pat Thai went into a 7eleven and bought a sandwich and a beer. Pat then sat on a curb across the road. He pointed the camera towards the 7eleven while he ate so that his viewers could enjoy watching people walking in and out of the store. There was no traffic on the roads so Noah was making good time. He figured he was only five minutes away when Pat Thai finished his sandwich and started drinking his beer. He started talking to his viewers again with slurred words, commenting on all the beautiful young Thai women walking by. If a beautiful Thai woman happened to stand still for a few minutes, he would zoom in and keep the camera on her the whole time. It was creepy.

When Noah was only a few minutes from Kao San Road, a young Thai woman stumbled towards 7eleven and sat on the steps outside. Even Pat Thai commented on how drunk she looked, as she rested her arms on her knees and hung her head low, with her hair dropping down over her face. To make matters worse, the woman was sitting with her legs wide open. Pat Thai zoomed in between her thighs. Her white panties were live on Youtube. Noah was watching the live stream, but he had to look away at this point. It was horrible and distasteful. *How is he getting away with this?* he wondered.

Suddenly Noah could hear a Thai man's voice on the live stream. He seemed irate. Pat Thai kept the camera focused on the white panties, but off camera he kept saying to the angry Thai man, "My pen rye", which even Noah knew meant 'No problem'. The Thai man's voice got louder and louder as he became more aggravated. Pat Thai turned the camera towards the man. He was a taxi driver standing in the middle of Kao San Road looking for falang customers. He started shouting at Pat Thai as he pointed at the drunken girl outside 7eleven.

"My pen rye," Pat Thai kept repeating.

He pointed the camera back to the girl and zoomed in on her panties again. The taxi driver moved towards Pat Thai and tried to grab the camera. There was a tussle and the camera seemed to fall to the ground. The live stream stopped abruptly.

Noah arrived at the top of Kao San Road right after the live stream ended. He paid the fare and jumped out of the taxi. He started running down Kao San Road, but the crowds were too thick. He had to dart in and out of little gaps between the crowds and then run when small pockets of space presented themselves. He passed two 7elevens before he finally found the one he was looking for. First Noah recognized the pathetic drunken girl on the steps. Then he looked to the other side of the street and saw Pat Thai and the taxi driver facing each other. The taxi driver was yelling at Pat Thai because he was filming the girl secretly, and Pat Thai was angry because the taxi driver broke his camera. A crowd started to gather around them as they argued. Their voices were getting louder and the taxi driver in particular looked like he was ready to start throwing punches. Sensing that a fight would break out any minute, Noah instinctively pushed his way through the crowd and stood between them, acting as peacemaker. The taxi driver stepped back and seemed happy to drop the matter. But then he looked at Pat Thai and let out an exaggerated laugh. Pat Thai took great offense to this. He suddenly sprung forward to attack the taxi driver, but fortunately Noah grabbed him and held him back. The taxi driver started laughing again. Pat Thai went crazy. He tried to push past Noah, but when he realized that he couldn't, he leant forward and spat at the taxi driver. Of course this enraged the Thai man. His eyes widened and it looked like he was ready to kill. He started walking slowly towards the two falangs with bad intentions. Noah pushed Pat Thai away and shouted, "Run!" The two falangs pushed through the crowd and escaped down a small alley. They sprinted as fast as they could and dared not look back, in fear that they might see a gang of Thai taxi drivers chasing after them. When they came out the other side of the alley, they turned left and continued running until they got to Soi Ram Butri. When they looked back, they were relieved to see that nobody was following them. They started walking away from the main road, away from danger, but they were both so out of breath that they couldn't say a single word to each other for a few minutes.

Eventually Pat Thai turned to Noah and said, "You're the guy from this morning."

"Right."

"Why did you help me?"

"Because you would have ended up in hospital or jail."

"I need a drink," Pat Thai announced.

"I'd say that's the last thing you need," Noah said, shaking his head in disgust as he thought about Pat Thai's dreadful behavior back on Kao San Road.

Pat Thai insisted on buying Noah a drink to thank him for his help. They sat down for a beer at a small vintage van that was converted into a street bar halfway down Soi Ram Butri. All the running seemed to have sobered Pat Thai up a bit.

"You followed me to Bangkok," he said, as he sipped his beer.

"Yes," Noah replied.

"You want me to delete the video."

"Right."

"Okay. Okay. I'll delete it. I should have deleted it this morning when you said you had a girlfriend back home."

Noah made a point of not thanking him. They sat in silence for several minutes before Noah turned to Pat Thai and said, "You know, it's not just about the video last night. You shouldn't be live streaming in bars in the first place, not to mention videoing drunk people on the street. I noticed that you hardly ever show your face."

Pat Thai nodded his head slightly, deep in thought.

"If you keep videoing people like that, you'll end up getting in trouble," Noah continued. "People come over here on holiday. They don't want to be on Youtube."

Pat Thai didn't reply immediately. He took a few minutes to reflect on things.

"You know, when I first started Youtube, I used to do these cool videos where I went off the beaten track and found amazing beaches and islands that hardly any Westerners even knew about. I used to do hotel reviews, interview local people and find nice cheap restaurants. That's when my channel was at its peak. I need to get back to that."

"Why did you get away from all that and start live streaming?" Noah asked.

"Because I started drinking more and I got lazy. You know, it's difficult to make a new video every day. Live streaming is much easier, but it makes a lot of people pissed off. It doesn't feel right."

Pat Thai agreed to delete all his live streams from his channel. He admitted that old live streams get hardly any views anyway so it wasn't a huge loss to him. Noah was happy to hear it. They shared a taxi back to Sukhumvit and then went their separate ways.

Noah and Andy returned to Pattaya the next day and carried on with their holiday. They spent one more night in Pattaya before they flew down south to Phuket and then back to Bangkok for the last few nights. But for Noah the trip was ruined. Not because of Pat Thai, but because every time he went out at night with Andy, he was constantly worried about being caught on camera by Youtubers. Now that he was conscious of it, he noticed loads of Western men walking around the entertainment areas in Pattaya, Phuket and Bangkok filming everything. He even became more worried when Andy told him that some Youtubers walk the streets and make videos with secret cameras. Noah had no intention of kissing another girl during his trip, but he hated the idea of being filmed in a girly bar or even walking along the street. One of the things he loved about Thailand was that he always felt a great sense of freedom there – what happens in Thailand stays in Thailand – but that was not the case anymore.

Bangkok Surprise

My last trip to Bangkok got off to a disastrous start. I was in Japan teaching English and I had a week off during the summer, so I headed to Thailand. It's only a six-hour flight from Tokyo to Bangok. I arrived on a hot and humid Saturday afternoon without a hint of jetlag. My Japanese bank card could not be used in other countries, so I knew I would have to use my English bank card. However, as soon as I passed immigration in Suvarnabhumi airport, I went to an ATM and it rejected my card. I tried a couple of other ATMs from different Thai banks, but the message 'Cannot complete transaction' kept coming up on the screen. I couldn't figure out what was happening. I had been to Thailand half a dozen times before, and my English cards had always worked. Then a horrible thought crossed my mind. I had been in Japan for over a year, and I had not used the card in all that time. I looked at the expiration date. My heart sank. The card had expired six months ago. I was screwed. I had a credit card, but it only had a one-thousand-pound limit, and I had maxed that out booking my flights and hotel, and buying bits and pieces online. It was a Saturday, so even if I used online banking to transfer money to pay off the credit card, it would take one working day to process. That meant I would not be able to use my credit card until Tuesday morning British time, Tuesday evening Thai time. I had three thousand baht in cash on me that I had exchanged in Tokyo. I figured if I took it easy I could make the three thousand baht last until Tuesday. My hotel was already paid for, so surely three thousand baht would be enough to get me three meals and a couple of beers a day. But it was so frustrating. During my previous trips to Thailand I was always on a tight budget. This time I actually had a lot of money, but I couldn't access it. I really didn't want to spend almost half of my trip on a tight budget. I wanted to enjoy myself.

I had a room booked in a hotel on Soi 4, Sukhumvit. Perhaps it would have been wise to try to figure out how to go there by bus or train to save myself a few quid, but I was stressed enough already so I took a taxi for five hundred baht. The room was nice. There was a big bed, a wide screen TV mounted to the wall and a wide-open space with a sofa and a coffee table to the side. During my previous trips to Thailand I always stayed in cheap guesthouses, so this was a big step up for me.

After I checked that everything was working in the room, I connected to the wifi and accessed my online banking. I paid off my one thousand pound credit card in one go. I knew that it wouldn't be processed until Tuesday, but I wanted to send the payment as early as possible anyway. Next, I wanted to call my bank but I didn't think I would get good call quality if I skyped them on the hotel wifi, so I decided to head out and find somewhere with an international call service. I found a small store on Soi 5 that offered international calls, though the rates were exorbitant. I called my bank's customer service, and predictably I heard an automated message say, 'All the operators are busy right now. Please hold. We thank you for your patience.' Then the classical music started. *This call is going to cost me a fortune,* I thought. After about ten minutes, I got through to an operator and I explained my situation. She was far from sympathetic. She simply told me that I had no other choice but to wait until Tuesday for my credit card payment to go through.

"I can't wait that long," I told her, trying to sound desperate. "Is there anything you can do to help me? Can you put a priority on the credit card payment and rush it through? Even if you could get it processed by Monday, it would be a big help."

"There's nothing I can do," she said. "Perhaps you can

contact family and they can send you money."

"I don't think they would be able to," I said hopelessly.

I really didn't want to reach out to my parents and ask them for help. Plus, I couldn't even imagine how they would get money to me during the weekend. I had never used Western Union before and I had no idea how it worked, and my parents definitely didn't know how to send money via Western Union. No, my parents couldn't help me this time.

I went back to my hotel room in a horrible mood. I just lay on my bed for over an hour and felt sorry for myself. By the time I snapped out of it, it was already dark outside. I was starving. I counted my money. I had a little over two thousand baht left. I went out to get dinner, but as I was walking along Soi 4 I saw another store offering international calls. I decided to give my bank another call. *There's no harm in trying again*, I thought. This time I ended up waiting almost half an hour for an operator. I was almost ready to give up when the classical music stopped and I was put through to an operator. Again, I explained my situation and pleaded with the operator to help me. At first she refused, but this operator was much more sympathetic than the last one. I told her that my parents would not be able to help me and that it would be difficult to wait until Tuesday to use my credit card. Suddenly the tone of her voice changed.

"Can I put you on hold for a few minutes?" she asked, sounding hopeful. "I want to see what my manager says about this situation."

I sat up straight and my heart started beating with excitement. *Perhaps I can have fun in Nana Plaza tonight after all,* I thought, with a big grin on my face. A few minutes later, the lovely operator came back to me and said that her manager had agreed to rush through my payment.

"You will be able to use your credit card in about an hour," she said.

"Oh my God! That's great news."

"But I must inform you that this is a once in a lifetime chance. Customers can only request this priority service one time. It's only for emergencies. Are you sure you want to use your one and only chance for this?"

"Yes," I replied, without hesitation.

The phone call cost me over five hundred baht, but I didn't care. It was worth it. I sat down for a meal in a restaurant on Soi 4, and while I was waiting for my food, all I could think was thank god I called customer service again.

After dinner I went back to my room to have a shower and change into clean clothes. Now all I needed was a wallet full of cash and I would be ready for a big night out. An hour had passed since my call with the bank, so I went downstairs and used the ATM right outside my hotel. This was a real make or break moment for my trip. If the customer service operator had made a mistake and wasn't able to prioritize my payment, I wouldn't be able to withdraw money and I would have to go back to my hotel for the night. I was almost shaking with anticipation as I put the card into the ATM and entered my password. Fortunately, I got a message saying 'Transaction Complete. Please take your cash and receipt.' I was delighted. What a horrible first day in Bangkok, but it was almost worth it for the rush of joy I felt when my card finally worked and I held twenty thousand baht in my hand.

I hurried towards Nana Plaza. I was in such a good mood that I even smiled at the ladyboy freelancers that lined the street. As I approached Nana, I saw a crowd of girls and ladyboys hanging around the entrance. When I reached the entrance to Nana Plaza, I was taken aback by the sight of a really tall ladyboy. She was wearing a sky-blue skimpy top (not much more than a bikini) with a matching hot pants and baseball cap. She had huge fake tits and long black hair down to her ass, but the most striking thing was her dark skin. She was clearly Thai, but her skin was almost black. I couldn't help but wonder if she had put on some kind of darkening cream to make her look like that. She caught me taking a second look at her. She gestured for me to come talk with her, but I shook my head quickly and rushed into Nana.

I had been to Nana Plaza about a dozen times before, but as I was walking around the ground floor I realized that this was my first time going there sober. It felt weird. Usually I would love the attention from the girls and I would just walk confidently into any bar, order a beer and scan the room for a girl I liked. But without a few drinks in me, I felt terribly uncomfortable walking around. There was a group of girls standing outside the first Go-go bar on the ground floor, and when I walked past, some of them stood in front of me and tried to get me to go into their bar. I just smiled awkwardly and walked around them as quickly as I could. I wanted to go into the bar, but I was too shy and uncomfortable. I kept walking and told myself that I would go into a bar upstairs instead. I hurried to the stairs at the back and went up to the second floor. Several tall ladyboys were waiting at the top of the stairs. I hurried passed them and veered left. More girls tried to get me to go into their bar, but I just kept walking and smiling like a fool. I was feeling increasingly uncomfortable being approached by all these women, so I kept walking faster and faster. I hurried up to the third floor, darted passed all the bars, girls and ladyboys before I finally decided to get out of there and take a few minutes to compose myself.

I felt much more comfortable when I got out of Nana Plaza

and walked towards my hotel. *I'm not going back there sober*, I told myself. I checked the time. It was already passed ten o' clock. If I sat in a quiet bar and drank beer until I was sufficiently drunk to tackle Nana again, it would be passed midnight. I wanted to get drunk and go back to Nana by eleven o' clock, so I headed to a 7eleven. I bought a big bottle of coke, plastic cups, a bag of ice and a small bottle of Sam Song (a cheap Thai rum). Back in my hotel I turned on Youtube and poured myself a rum and coke. I had drunk Sam Song loads of times before on the islands down south. I knew that I could drink it fast if I mixed it with enough coke. By eleven o' clock I had finished everything and I was ready to head out again.

This time I felt much more comfortable walking passed the freelancers around the entrance of Nana. The rum had kicked in and I felt great. I strolled into Nana Plaza feeling confident and carefree. I went upstairs and I let myself be dragged into the first Go-go bar I passed. I sat in the back, away from the stage. After I ordered a beer, two girls sat either side of me and tried to spark up a conversation. I was polite to them both, but they soon realized that I was not in the least bit interested in either of them. In truth, they both looked too skinny and young. A few minutes later, another girl came over, but I wasn't interested in her because she was really plain looking. I had rejected the advances of three girls in quick succession, so the Mamasan – a short, chubby woman in her forties - came over and asked what kind of girl I was looking for.

"I'm not sure," I said. "I just came to have a look and drink a beer."

"You no want lady?" she asked, surprised.

"Maybe. I'm not sure yet. Just looking first."

I didn't want to tell her my taste in women because I knew she would start sending more girls over to talk with me. Fortunately, she was not a pushy Mamasan. She went back to her seat at the end of the bar and let me alone to enjoy my beer in peace. After that, the girls on the stage waved and winked at me a lot, and when the girls passed my table they waved at me and smiled, but nobody approached me. That suited me fine, because half way through my first beer I realized that I was not particularly attracted to any of the girls in the bar. However, it was a nice little spot to drink. That's why I stayed for a second and third beer.

After I paid my bill in the first bar, I went up to the third floor and ventured into a large bar at the top of the stairs. I had never been in there before, so I was surprised to see that there was a row of glass shower booths above the stage. When I was ordering a beer from the waitress, I asked, "What are they for?"

"They for shower show. It start in five minutes," she

answered.

The show started a little late, but it was worth the wait. Three girls went into the booths and started washing themselves seductively with lots and lots of suds. They were a little far away so I couldn't appreciate their bodies fully, but all the girls looked beautiful. While I was watching the show, one of the other Go-go girls sat alongside me and asked, "My friends very sexy, right?"

She introduced herself as Nan. She was curvy and she had wavy brown hair down to her shoulders. Nan was not particularly beautiful, but she had unnaturally long fake eyelashes that really caught my attention. Perhaps they would look stupid in broad daylight, but in the dark setting of a Go-go bar they made her look glamorous. I bought Nan a lady drink and we watched the shower show come to an end.

"Will you be doing the shower show next?" I asked her.

"No," Nan said. "You buy me lady drink, so I sit with you."

Nan's lady drink was a small glass of coke that apparently also contained whiskey. She drank it down in two big gulps, and after a few minutes she asked me to buy her another one. I didn't want to waste money on another lady drink, but I did want to barfine her. We agreed a price of one thousand five hundred baht for short time. I thought that was a bit steep. I told Nan that I always used to pay one thousand baht for short time, but she convinced me that prices had gone up in the past few years. I didn't argue with her because I figured I could make up the five hundred baht by taking her back to my hotel instead of one of the short time rooms in Nana. But as soon as we left the bar, Nan said that she didn't want to go back to my hotel.

"Why not?" I asked. "I stay in hotel near here. It's only one minute away."

"No, please. Let's use room downstairs," she said. "It nice room and cheap. Please."

The best thing about my hotel was that it was within a stone's throw of Nana, so I thought I could bring girls back there easily. I hated going into those dodgy short time rooms. God knows what's crawling on the mattresses! But there was not much I could do. I had already paid Nan's barfine and I wanted to be with her, so I reluctantly gave in. It was short time alright; we were finished within twenty minutes, showers included.

I had drunk four beers and the small bottle of rum, so I was now feeling quite drunk. I could walk straight and talk normally, but my head was spinning a bit. Even so, there was no chance of me going back to my room yet. The night was still young. After I said goodbye to Nan, I went down to the ground floor and sat at one of the open air bars in the middle of Nana

Plaza. I talked to a couple of the girls behind the bar and bought them drinks. While I was talking with them, I started to think about what I wanted to do for the rest of the night. Nana was closing and I had no interest in sleeping with another woman. My old demons started speaking to me. *Yaba. Yaba. Why don't you do Yaba? This is a perfect chance. You are in Bangkok. You won't have this chance again for a long time. Go for it. Why not?* I had smoked yaba on my last two trips to Thailand. When I decided to come to Thailand this time, I swore to myself that I wouldn't smoke because I knew it would ruin my whole trip. I would end up spending most of my time holed up in a room doing nothing. But I was drunk now and suddenly yaba seemed very appealing. I wanted to have fun. I had money to burn. I wanted a wild night in Bangkok. The problem was that I had no idea where to get yaba. The last few times I did it, I was drinking with bar girls after Nana closed and they invited me back to their room to smoke with them. *How do I find a girl who smokes yaba?* I wondered.

When I left Nana Plaza at two o' clock, I could think about nothing other than yaba. I walked up and down Soi 4 for about half an hour with the silly hope that a freelancer would just walk up to me and ask me to smoke with her. Of course that didn't happen. My last few beers had kicked in by now and I was really drunk. I knew that yaba smokers are usually really skinny, so I decided I would just walk up to the next really skinny freelancer I saw and ask her if she does yaba. But that's not exactly what ended up happening. When I walked to the top of Soi 4, a freelancer in a very tight-fitting red dress stood directly in front of me and smiled.

"I go with you," she said, in a sweet voice.

The tight red dress fitted awkwardly on her because she had love handles and a slightly protruding belly. She wore thick makeup, but there was a beautiful round face behind it all. There was absolutely nothing about her appearance to suggest that she smoked, yet I decided to try my luck.

I waited for a few people to pass, and then I leant into her and whispered, "I want to smoke yaba."

She didn't seem in the least bit surprised by my question.

"You want to smoke with me?" she asked.

"Yes," I said. "But I just want to smoke. I don't want sex or anything, so I can't pay you. But I can pay for yaba and we can share."

"Okay. We go smoke," she said. "We go to my room with taxi."

In the taxi I came to know that her name was Coco. Apart from exchanging names, we barely said another word to each other for the rest of the fifteen-minute taxi ride. I really was not interested in Coco. I just wanted to smoke with her for a few hours and then leave. The taxi stopped outside a large apartment building. Before we went inside, I turned to Coco and asked, "Don't we need a bottle to make a gun out of, and foil from a chewing gum pack to make a boat with?"

"I have everything. Don't worry," she assured me.

The apartment building had an open entrance, but there was a reception desk near the elevator. Coco brought me there and asked me to pay five hundred baht.

"For what?" I asked.

"For room."

"But you said you have a room."

"I have, but I stay with brother. We need other room."

She never mentioned that back in Sukhumvit, and it struck me as odd that we could rent an apartment for one night. I was a bit annoyed and confused, but yaba was almost within reach so I paid the five hundred baht quickly and followed Coco to the elevator. Now that we were inside the building, I could see that the place was old and run down. In the elevator I asked Coco, "Are you sure you have yaba? I don't want to wait for a long time."

"Yes, my brother have," she said. "No worry."

Our room was on the eight floor. It was nicer than I expected. It had a similar layout to my hotel room, but there was no sofa, and everything else looked cheaper and older, especially the TV and the wardrobe.

"I go buy from my brother now," Coco said. "I need money."

I gave her three thousand baht to buy ten yaba pills. As she reached for the door, I asked her, "Where's your brother's room?"

"At end of this hall," she said. "I come back very quickly."

I didn't mind being left alone in the room at first because I had no drugs on me, I had no drugs in my system, and as far as I knew there were no drugs in the room. But ten minutes passed without any sign of Coco, and I started to wonder if I had been set up. It suddenly dawned on me how stupid and naïve I had been. I gave three thousand baht to a complete stranger and let her walk off with the money. Then I realized that I had no proof that Coco really did have a room in this building with her brother. That could have all been part of the set up. It also occurred to me that Coco had no incentive to come back to me. I already told her that I didn't want to have sex with her and that I wouldn't pay her anything. She already had my drug money, so she could just use it for herself rather than coming back and sharing the drugs with me. Another ten minutes passed and there was still no sign of her. I lay down on the bed and told myself to forget about yaba and the three thousand baht. I was starting to nod off when I heard a quiet knock on the door. It was Coco.

Coco had changed into shorts and a nicely fitting white tank top. I guess she didn't want to spend the rest of the night squeezed into the red dress. She was carrying a small makeup bag in one hand and a small plastic bag in the other. She knelt down on the floor next to the bedside locker. I sat on the bed.

"Where were you? I was waiting for a long time."

"Sorry. Sorry," she said, as she took out two bottles of water from the plastic bag. "I take shower and change clothes."

She also took out two small packs of chocolate milk from the plastic bag and handed one to me.

"Drink this before we smoke," she said. "When we smoke, maybe you not eat for a long time. This good for your body."

Chocolate milk was the last thing I wanted, but I drank it because I was touched that she was trying to take care of me. As Coco was opening up the makeup bag, she looked up at me and said, "My brother no have yaba, sorry."

I took a deep breath to compose myself. I didn't want to lose my temper.

"What do you mean he doesn't have yaba? You mean we have to wait?"

"No, he cannot get tonight so I buy ice."

Coco reached into her makeup bag and took out a small

plastic ziplock bag about half the size of a playing card. I had never smoked or even seen ice (crystal meth) before. Coco handed me the bag so that I could have a closer look. There was a bunch of tiny crystals of various sizes at the bottom of the bag. The first thing that came to mind was that there was such a tiny amount of the stuff.

"How much was this?" I asked.

"Three thousand five hundred baht," Coco answered.

"For this?" I was shocked.

"This one gram. My brother give good price," she said. "It not like yaba. This small but it last long time. I show you. Don't worry."

Coco placed the bag of ice on the bedside locker, and then she took out a glass pipe that was connected to a small glass bong. She poured some water into the bong and then used a tweezers to pick out a crystal from the bag. Then she dropped the crystal into the hole in the glass sphere at the end of the pipe. Coco took out four lighters from her makeup bag and tested them all. She handed me the bong and the lighter with the smallest flame.

"I've never smoked ice before," I admitted.

"Okay. I help you," she said very kindly.

I held the bong up to my mouth while Coco moved the flame of the lighter slowly back and forth under the glass sphere.

After a few seconds, the sphere filled up with smoke and I inhaled quickly. I have the ability to inhale a lot of smoke (especially at the start of a session), so I kept breathing in for more than a minute. "Oh my god!" Coco said several times, surprised by how much I could inhale.

Eventually I held up my right hand to signal for Coco to stop the flame. When she pulled away the lighter, the smoke kept coming for a few seconds so I had to keep inhaling otherwise it would have been wasted. When I exhaled the smoke, I got a weird stale taste in my mouth.

"How is it?" Coco asked.

"It's okay," I said. "But the taste is weird. Yaba tastes much better."

"Yes, yaba taste good but very cheap and dirty drug. This little bit expensive but very pure and good."

Coco handed me the bong again.

"You do," I said, trying not to be selfish.

"You do one more time, then I do."

I noticed that Coco didn't put a new crystal in this time. I looked at the glass sphere closely.

"It's all gone," I said.

Coco pointed at some grey patches in the sphere and said, "This ice too. There a lot left."

While I held the bong to my mouth again, Coco held the flame up to one of the gray patches on the right wall of the sphere. Suddenly smoke started to fill the sphere again and I had to inhale quickly. Over half the sphere was covered in these gray patches, so even after I took another big hit, there was still plenty left for Coco. I was amazed that such a tiny crystal could last such a long time. I held up the small plastic bag again. I counted over a dozen small crystals and a couple of big ones. Suddenly it didn't seem like such a small amount after all. I remembered that Coco had mentioned that she paid three thousand five hundred baht for the ice. I had only given her three thousand baht, so I took out my wallet and handed her five hundred baht.

The ice took affect almost immediately. The drowsiness from the alcohol was gone, my mind was clear, I felt energized, and I was very happy and excited to be in a Bangkok apartment with Coco. She looked beautiful and sexy now, and she seemed like a genuinely warm and caring person. We smoked a few crystals quickly to get an initial rush, and then over the next hour we smoked slowly and talked more. Coco told me that she used to work in a Go-go bar in Nana Plaza, but she hated dancing on the stage and trying to get lady drinks from customers. She said she was much happier as a freelancer.

"I very lazy, so I go Nana 2 AM every night," she explained, "and if I no have customer at 3 AM, I go home. No problem."

"2 AM? Jesus! Do you smoke a lot?"

"Only when customer want."

All the girls say they only smoke when customers want to, but I actually believed Coco. Her face looked full and healthy, and she was carrying a few pounds around her waist.

When the morning sun started to shine through the gap in the curtains, Coco placed the ice and the bong under the bed.

"Now we rest for a while," she said.

We both lay down on the bed facing each other. The night had turned out much better than I had expected. I experienced ice for the first time and I found a nice, beautiful woman. I pulled Coco close to me and kissed her. We kissed softly and passionately for a few minutes, and then she pulled back and said, "When I meet you in Sukhumvit, you say you no want me."

"I was stupid and drunk," I said. "Sorry."

"You want me now?" she asked, with a cheeky grin.

"Yes," I answered quickly, pulling her close again.

We kissed and caressed each other. Her breasts were larger and softer than I had imagined. I couldn't take my hands off of them. When Coco reached down and felt my erection, she told me to get a condom.

"I don't' have," I said, still undecided about how far I was willing to go without protection.

We made out some more and then Coco stopped.

"I go my room and get condom," she said. "I come back quickly."

That seemed like a good idea. She put on her tank top and rushed out the door. For some reason, I suddenly wanted proof that she was really going to her and her brother's room at the end of the hall. I jumped out of bed and hurried to the door. I slowly opened the door and discreetly watched Coco walk down the hall and disappear into the last apartment. It was a relief to see that she was telling the truth.

How long does it take to get a condom? I kept asking myself. Twenty minutes passed and there was still no sign of Coco. I wanted to open the door and see if she was coming, but I was conscious of the fact that there was a small bag of drugs under my bed. Around the half hour mark, I heard a door closing down the hall and then there was a knock on my door. I couldn't be annoyed with Coco for taking so long because we were about to have sex. I just had to forget about it. Probably thanks to the ice, sex with Coco was amazing. Meth heightens your emotions and creates bonds between people, so I felt incredibly close (almost in love) with Coco. When we finished, I had a quick shower and then we started smoking again. Then, surprisingly, at about 8 AM, Coco said she had to go back to her room to have a shower.

"Have a shower here," I said.

Coco insisted that she needed to shower in her room because she needed to use some cosmetics, and she wanted to change into new clothes. I really didn't want her to go. I mean, she took twenty minutes to get a condom, so I dreaded to think how long she would take to have a shower, change her clothes and do god knows what else. Coco could see that I wasn't happy. She kissed me and told me not to be sad.

"I come back quickly," she assured me. "Rest now and don't smoke too much."

This time Coco took the room key with her. I looked at my watch soon after she left. It was 7:30 AM. *I'll give her until eight o' clock*, I thought. *Surely that is enough time to have a shower and get ready.* Unsurprisingly, Coco didn't return by eight o' clock. I hated waiting in the room alone with drugs. I worried about what I would do if someone came banging on the door. I could flush the ice down the toilet, but there was no good way to get rid of the bong. The longer I waited for Coco, the more I worried that something bad was about to happen. I was in a perilous spot – sitting alone with meth under my bed in a part of Bangkok that I didn't know, waiting for a girl I hardly knew. It was now half past eight. I started to give serious thought to the possibility that Coco had called the police on me. *Why else would she be staying away for this long?* I kept asking myself. *She'll probably get a reward for reporting a falang, or a cut of the bribe that the police will ask from me.* The door was not double locked, so it would be easy for the police to kick it down. And of course Coco had the keys, so she could just let them in. I stood by the door and listened for sounds. I heard whispers outside the door, I thought, but perhaps it was the morning wind blowing through the narrow hallway. There was a lot of movement outside because it was the morning and people were leaving for work. It was horrible listening to every voice and footstep, dreading that every new sound might be the start of a police raid.

I waited for Coco unit 9:30 AM. I refused to wait anymore. I was worried about the police coming to the room, but I also felt horribly disrespected that Coco kept me waiting for hours without any reason. I refused to keep waiting for her indefinitely. I hid the ice and the bong under the pillows, and then I hurried out the door. As I walked up a narrow soi towards the main road, I kept looking back, worried that I was being watched or followed. I only started to relax when I was in the back of a taxi on the way to Sukhumvit. I didn't feel great about doing a runner on Coco, but she left me no choice. I mean, two hours is a reasonable amount of time to wait for somebody who only went down the hall for a shower. The only small regret I had was that I didn't leave Coco a thousand baht for the time we spent together, but then again I did leave her half a gram of ice.

When I got back to my hotel room, I lay in bed for most of the day. I didn't feel like doing anything. I watched some TV shows on my laptop for a while, but I can never really focus on TV after a meth session. There was no chance of me getting a wink of sleep after a night on ice, and my appetite was shot too. I felt awake and full of energy, but I didn't want to go out into the sun. Just staying in my room, lying on my bed suited me fine.

Time flew and it was soon dark outside. I went to Nana Plaza at about 10 PM, and over the next few hours I had half a dozen beers in several Go-go bars. Shortly after midnight I wanted a change of scenery. I left Nana and looked for a quieter place to drink. I walked to the top of Soi 4, turned right and found an alco cart in front of the Majestic Suites and Nana Post Office. There were three stools at the bar, but there were also three plastic tables with chairs placed along the sidewalk. I sat down and ordered a beer. I was the only customer. The owner of the alco cart was a Thai woman in her forties. She was shabbily dressed and she paid no attention to her appearance, so I knew that she was one of the few women around Nana who was not interested in going with a falang. She sat with me and made small talk, perhaps to practice her English. It was nice to talk with her. Even though I was on my seventh beer, I felt perfectly sober. It's hard to get drunk after a meth session. However, I was starting to feel tired – not sleepy, but a strange fatigue was taking hold of my body and making me feel sluggish. It wasn't a bad feeling, but the problem was that I knew I wouldn't be able to sleep anytime soon. There was still meth in my blood. I decided it would be best to smoke again, stay up during the day and then hopefully sleep tomorrow night.

Once again I was faced with the problem of finding someone to smoke with. In hindsight it was a really stupid thing to do, but I turned to the alco cart woman and said quietly, "I want to smoke yaba. Do you know anyone who smokes?"

This woman didn't know my name or where I was staying, so I figured if she pulled back in disgust at my question, I could just apologize and do a runner. In fact, when she heard my question, she threw her head back and started laughing.

"You want to smoke?" she asked. "Yaba not good. You should be careful."

"I know," I said. "But do you know anyone who I can smoke with?"

Her eyes squinted slightly as she tried to think of someone who could help me.

"I know one person," she said. "She a ladyboy. You want me to call her?"

"A ladyboy?"

"Yes."

I hesitated. There was a clear path between me and yaba, and I couldn't resist the temptation, even if there was a ladyboy standing in the way. I told the alco cart lady to call the ladyboy. After a quick phone call, she said, "She come in five minutes. Wait here."

I ordered another beer.

The ladyboy came before the beer did. She was tall and I could see straight away that she had breast and butt implants. Her body was amazing, but her face looked too artificial. Her lips looked swollen and her eyes looked unnaturally big. She spoke with the alco cart lady briefly and then sat alongside me.

"You want to smoke?" she asked, in a surprisingly natural feminine voice.

"Yes." I said.

"What you want smoke?"

"Yaba."

"And you want sex too?"

"No sex, just smoke."

"Why I go with you just to smoke? I need customer."

"I will pay for the candy and we can smoke together."

"I don't need. I already smoke. I need customer."

"Okay. I will pay for yaba and I will give you one thousand bath too."

We were both happy with that deal, so I paid my bill and I followed the ladyboy to the side of the road, where we jumped into a taxi.

In the back of the taxi, I asked, "How far is your room?"

"Not far," she said.

"By the way, what's your name?"

"Dick," she replied, with a straight face.

"Dick?" I laughed "Really? Why do you have that name?"

"I don't know," she said. "My ex-husband give it to me."

I thought she would give me a suggestive or naughty look when we talked about her name, but her face was completely expressionless. She went on to tell me that she used to live in England with her falang husband, but he recently died so she had to return to Thailand and start working again.

I couldn't believe my eyes when I stepped out of the taxi. I was standing right in front of Coco's apartment building again. I followed Dick passed the reception desk straight to the elevator. Fortunately, her room was on the twelfth floor, not the eight. When we entered the room, I was surprised to see two other ladyboys sitting on the floor, drinking beer and playing with their phones. They were Dick's roommates. Conveniently, one of the roommates was a yaba dealer. Throughout the night I ended up buying twenty yaba pills and sharing them with the three ladyboys. They treated me well and I felt comfortable smoking with them, but soon after the sun came up, I started to get restless. Coco was only four floors below me and I knew which room she was staying in. *Why not go knock on her door?* I thought. Maybe it was the yaba talking, but I missed Coco and I wanted to be with her again. I wanted to apologize for doing a runner and give her money for the night we spent together. I thanked the three ladyboys for letting me hang out in their room and I gave Dick a thousand baht, as promised. I told her that I was tired and just wanted to go back to my hotel.

When I got into the elevator, I felt nervous and excited at the thought of seeing Coco again. I desperately hoped that she wouldn't be angry with me. I wanted to kiss her and feel her large, soft breasts again. The elevator stopped on the eight floor and I got a fright when I saw a Thai family of four (a mother, a father, and two boys between six and ten years old) standing right in front of the elevator door. They had to stand aside to let me pass. First, I noticed that the two boys were dressed in a cute school uniform with grey shorts, long white socks and a white shirt. The father was also wearing a white shirt, and he looked like he was off to work for the day. It was a lovely scene of a young Thai family. Of course I had to take a look at the mother to see what she looked like, and my jaw almost dropped when I saw that it was Coco. She looked right passed me. Fortunately, I had the presence of mind to keep walking and leave her and her family alone. I looked back and saw the elevator close on Coco and her family. I stopped in the hallway and said aloud, "Fucking hell!"

I was dumbfounded. She didn't live with her brother at the end of the hall after all. She lived with her husband and two sons. I looked at the time. It was half eight. Now I understood why she had left me alone for so long the previous morning. She probably had to make breakfast for her family, get her children ready and bring them to school. I felt terrible. All I could do was walk to the end of the hall and slip the one thousand baht that I owed her under the door.

Pattaya Youtuber

When I landed in Thailand, I got a taxi straight to Pattaya. I had no interest in Bangkok. The taxi driver dropped me off at a bar I knew on Soi Bukhao called 'Whoopers'. I was expecting a warm welcome when I walked in, but all I got was the standard 'Sabaidee' greeting from the two staff behind the bar. I walked out the back to find Craig, the owner of the bar. He was kneeling down and cleaning the dirt off the wheels of his bicycle.

"I'm back," I said, reaching down to shake his hand.

"So you are," he mumbled, as he held out his wet hand.

I must say, I was a little offended that he didn't show a bit more enthusiasm about my arrival. I mean, we had spent countless nights getting pissed together in his bar. I thought he would have at least cracked a smile when he saw me.

Craig stood up and asked, "How long has it been?"

"Three months," I said. "Nothing has changed I see, except you've put on a bit of weight."

Craig wasn't one for banter when he was sober. I should have known better than to take the piss out of him before he had a few drinks in him.

"I've actually lost weight, ya cheeky cunt," Craig retorted, and then he grabbed his huge belly with two hands.

Craig was a fat, bald fellow English man in his early fifties. He moved to Pattaya about ten years ago and set up this bar/guesthouse.

"Have you rooms?" I asked.

"I do."

"And can I pay monthly like the last time?"

"You can, but you still owe me four thousand baht. Remember the tab you built up in the bar before you fucked off last time?"

I was kind of hoping he would have forgotten about that. I took out my wallet and started counting out twelve thousand baht – four thousand for the tab and eight thousand for the room. I followed Craig to the bar.

"How long are you staying for this time?" he asked, as he wrote me out a receipt.

"Not sure," I said. "Hopefully for a very long time. I set up a

Youtube channel called 'Pattaya Youtuber'."

"You too?" Craig said, rolling his eyes. "That's all Pattaya needs, another Youtuber."

My room was on the third floor. It was a decent enough room for the money. It had a nice shiny tiled floor, freshly painted walls, a double bed, a small fridge, a desk and chair, a bathroom and a tiny balcony overlooking Soi Buakhao. As soon as I got into the room, I had a shower and put on fresh clothes. I felt surprisingly good after my long journey. I was ready to make my first Youtube video. I took out my phone and started filming my room, explaining the price, the facilities and the location. I kept filming as I walked downstairs and showed the bar and where it was located on Soi Buakhao. I stopped filming and watched the video as I walked along the street. I noticed that the camera was shaking a bit, but it wasn't too bad. I just wanted to make simple videos quickly without worrying about the quality too much; that way I would be able to make videos every day. I started recording again when I entered a 7eleven. I filmed every corner of the store, explaining the prices of loads of items from beer to coffee to shampoo. I also introduced some interesting crisp flavors on sale in 7eleven, such as green curry and crab curry. I filmed myself buying a couple of beers and a sandwich, and fortunately the cashier didn't mind being on camera. I didn't bother telling him that he would be on Youtube within a couple of hours. I finished the video by walking back to my room and opening a nice cold beer. As soon as I stopped filming, I transferred the videos onto my laptop and started editing.

I must admit, I am shit at editing videos. I don't have the patience for it. Some Youtubers have degrees in media and film, so their videos are full of fancy editing, but I was going for the rough and ready style. Cut, cut, stick it all together, thumbnail and upload. Simple. But even that took me well over an hour. I was happy enough with the video, and while I was waiting for it to upload, I got the idea to make it the first video in a series called 'I left my job and moved to Pattaya'. I was delighted with myself. I figured that video title would grab people's attention and make them click, and at the end of the day, that's the name of the game.

I already had thirty subscribers. When I was back in England, I made thirty Gmail accounts in preparation for this day. I also had a VPN program that allowed me to go online with IP addresses from dozens of countries all around the world. For almost an hour I signed into these different accounts and clicked on my Youtube video. I made sure to let the whole video play each time to show Youtube that my video held viewers' attention. I also used an IP address from a different country each time to trick

Youtube into thinking my video was going global. I clicked the like button thirty times and I left about a dozen comments. I even clicked on popular falang Youtubers in Pattaya right after I watched my video to make Youtube think that people who liked their videos also liked mine. I did all of this so that Youtube's mysterious algorithm would favor my video and put it onto people's main page. After about an hour of signing in and out of accounts, I got a cool beer from the fridge and opened the analytics page on my channel. I had used every trick I knew, so now all I could do was sit back and hope for the best.

I pressed refresh on the page several times but nothing was happening. There was no activity, no views, and of course no new subscribers. Nothing. One hour, two hours passed without a single person watching my video. I thought you could throw up any old shit about Pattaya and people would lap it up, but apparently not. I was devastated. I needed to make this work. I only had a couple of grand in my bank account. I could make that stretch maybe three months at a push, but I wanted to stay in Pattaya much longer than that. I needed to get views quickly, grow my channel and start making money.

In the late evening I had a quick nap and then headed out for dinner as it was getting dark. I checked Youtube every five minutes, but I was still not getting any views. I stopped at a cheap restaurant I knew down the road and ordered a curry and beer. It was one of those small restaurants you find all over Thailand – blue plastic tables and chairs, a small open kitchen at the back, four small fans on the walls, and a fridge in the corner with beer and coke. While I was waiting for my food, I took out my phone and started making a list of the videos I wanted to make in my 'I left my job and moved to Pattaya' series. All in all, I had spent about ten months of my life in Pattaya over the past five years, so I knew the place better than most. I wanted to use my knowledge to make helpful, informative videos. But there were already thousands of Pattaya related videos on Youtube. It was hard to think up of original ideas for videos. I strained my brain thinking of new and creative ideas, but in the end I had to tell myself *Don't over think this. Just make videos about the normal things you do when you first arrive in Pattaya.* When I started thinking in these terms, it was easy to make a list of topics for videos – 'buying a sim card with phone data', 'renting a motorbike', 'best bars', 'cheap places to eat', 'favorite places away from the tourist areas', 'best places to meet women', 'street food'. Easy! I had my first week of videos planned in about five minutes.

After dinner, I went to a popular bar I knew off of Soi Buakhao. It was owned by a Mancunian. They played good English rock, and it was always full of falangs and beautiful Thai women. It was still early, so there were a couple of empty seats at the bar. I sat down and ordered a beer. I didn't recognize anyone in the bar at first, but after I ordered my second beer I headed for the bathroom in the back, and on my way I spotted a popular Youtuber called 'Beach Boy'. He was based in Pattaya and he had about fifty thousand subscribers – that's quite good on the Thailand scene. Beach Boy was in his fifties and he was sitting with two other falangs around his age. They were all holding up their phones and talking into their cameras, live streaming on Youtube. When I went back to my seat at the bar, I took out my phone and put on Beach Boy's live stream. I left a comment saying that I was in the same bar. Fortunately, he read my comment and invited me over. The three lads were almost twice my age, but they were all from England and we got on great. I was live on their channels, so I took the chance to mention that I was also a Youtuber. I said the name of my channel and the three lads urged their viewers to subscribe.

"Subscribe to the 'Pattaya Youtuber'," Beach Boy kept telling his viewers. "Help the poor lad out. He only has thirty subscribers, and they are probably all his friends and family."

It worked. Within half an hour I was up to two hundred subscribers. I was delighted. To be honest, I was very jealous of the three lads because they could live stream on Youtube. Live streaming is a great way to get extra money because viewers can donate money to your channel during the stream. It's a great money maker, but you need to have a thousand subscribers before you are eligible to live stream on Youtube. I was still a long way off that number.

For the next couple of weeks I stuck with my 'I left my job and moved to Pattaya' series and made a video every day, but I wasn't making much progress. I was only getting about five new subscribers a day, and each video only had a couple of hundred views. Those numbers wouldn't be so bad if I was at home living with my parents, but I was in Pattaya burning through money. I was out every night drinking heavily and barfining women regularly. I was desperate to get to a thousand subscribers quickly so that I could start live streaming and hopefully get some donations from my subscribers. But at the rate of five new subscribers a day, I'd be back in England by the time I got to a thousand. That was a depressing thought. I was sick of working as a restaurant manager back in the UK. I didn't want to go back to that mundane life. Something had to change, so I considered making different kinds of videos. My first month in my room above Whoopers bar was coming to an end, and the numbers of views and subscribers on my Youtube channel were disappointingly low. I was seriously considering packing up and making travel vlogs all around

Thailand, but then a breakfast with a bar girl completely changed everything for me.

When I barfine a girl, I always take her for short time. It's much cheaper than long time, and I am usually happy to see the back of her as soon as we finish the business. But on this occasion, I took the girl back to my room at about 3 AM, and after we finished everything, she asked if it was okay to stay. When we woke up in the morning, I was feeling generous and I asked her to join me for breakfast. I filmed the meal with her and uploaded it to Youtube straight away, with the title 'Breakfast with a Pattaya Bar Girl'. The video blew up! It got ten thousand views in two days, and thanks to that video, my other videos got extra views and I got about three hundred new subscribers. Now I knew the key to becoming a popular Pattaya Youtuber - show girls in your videos. From then on, I went to great lengths to include an attractive girl in every video I made. Whenever I was looking for a place to eat dinner, I walked the streets for up to an hour looking for a place with a hot waitress. Then I filmed her briefly while I was in the restaurant and used her as the thumbnail for the video. It always worked. Having a beautiful woman in the thumbnail is the best way to get views. I started doing reviews of hotels with attractive receptionists. I even found a few sexy food vendors and made a video about them. I never asked any of the women for their permission because I didn't need to. It's perfectly legal to film people in public places and stick it up on Youtube. It's the modern world.

Towards the end of my second month in Pattaya, I reached a thousand subscribers and I was now eligible to live stream on Youtube. I must admit, now that I could live stream, I wasn't really interested in making videos anymore. I was sick of thinking of ideas for the videos and the hours of editing involved. Live streaming suited me much better. As soon as I got word that I could start live streaming, I went downstairs and told Craig the good news. I told him that I wanted to live stream from his bar, and that I wanted something in return for my efforts.

"It will be good promotion for your bar," I told him.

"How many viewers do you expect to get?" he asked, not looking very enthusiastic about my offer.

"A couple of hundred," I answered, plucking the number out of thin air.

"If there are more than two hundred viewers, you can have a couple of free beers during the live stream," he said, as if he was doing me a huge favor. "But only one or two. Don't be taking the piss."

That seemed a fair deal to me, so we shook on it.

I started my first ever live stream on a Friday night in Whoopers bar at about 9 PM. It got off to a slow start. I only had eight viewers. In hindsight, I picked the wrong time. It was the early afternoon in the UK and the early morning in America, so most of my subscribers were probably at work. Plus, the bar was dead. There were a couple of decent looking girls behind the bar, but apart from me there were only two other customers. I sat at the bar alone and spoke into the camera about what I had been getting up to in Pattaya recently. I wasn't talking long when the questions started coming in through the comment section. The very few viewers I had were a very curious bunch. They asked me loads of questions about food, weather, current affairs, bars and girls in Pattaya. I was having fun answering their questions, but the numbers of viewers stayed very low. For the first thirty minutes I had between only twenty to forty viewers at any one time, so Craig refused to give me a free beer. I figured people were not interested in watching me sit alone in a quiet bar, so I hit the streets in search of something more exciting. I'm not a shy guy, but even I felt very awkward pointing my phone at myself and talking into the camera as I walked along Beach Road and Second Road. I felt very self-conscious.

As I was walking the streets of Pattaya, the numbers of

viewers started to creep up steadily. I told my viewers that once I hit the one-hundred mark, I would go to a girly bar on Walking Street. I soon hit the mark so I jumped into the very next girly bar I saw. The girls seemed a bit put off by the camera. They let me sit down and order a beer, but none of the girls came over to talk with me. Still, the girls were in the background of my video and the scene looked lively, so it made for a much better live stream. I stayed in the bar for a couple of hours and my viewer count hovered above one hundred and twenty the whole time. I was happy with that for my first live stream, considering much more popular Youtubers like 'Beach Boy' only got about three hundred viewers.

For the next couple of weeks I live streamed every night, walking the streets, jumping from bar to bar. People seemed to like my content. I was getting almost a hundred new subscribers a day. The money from Youtube wasn't good because the videos that I had uploaded were not getting many views, nor were the live streams that I uploaded after the event. But I was getting some Super Chats during each live stream. People often sent me a few quid for a beer or a meal. It averaged out to about twenty US dollars per live stream, but then Youtube took a thirty percent cut of that. I also set up a Paypal account and included it in the description of every video so that viewers could send me donations. The Super Chats and Paypal donations were paying for my food and a few beers every day so I was happy.

Though live streaming did help my channel grow considerably, there were times when I wanted to pack it all in and go back to editing videos. Live streaming caused me a lot of awkwardness and difficulty almost every day. For example, sometimes I would go into a bar, sit down, and before I could order a drink, the Mamasan would come over and ask me to leave. They were afraid that I would scare off customers, and of course some of the girls in the bar didn't want to be on Youtube because they probably had several boyfriends in other countries. The first few times this happened, I argued with the Mamasan and told her that she was being unreasonable, but it got me nowhere.

"No video in bar," the Mamasan would repeat over and over again until I left.

One night I was live streaming in a bar, sitting in the corner with a beer, and two huge older Americans walked in. Before they even reached the bar, one of them came over to me and said aggressively, "You can't film in here."

"Why not?" I asked, looking up at his quadruple chin.

"This is a bar. You can't film in here," he repeated, towering over me.

I looked at the comment section on my live stream. My

viewers were loving the confrontation, while I was shitting myself. This guy was much taller and heavier than me.

"I'm just filming my face," I said. "Nobody else."

He looked down at my phone and said, "No you're not. You can see half the bar on the screen."

"It's pointing only at me. Nobody else can be seen if they don't walk into shot."

"But the entrance to the bar is on the screen, so when I walked in, I was in shot, right?"

"For a second, perhaps."

"I don't want to be filmed," he shouted. "Turn it off or leave."

"Who are you to say that?" I said. "You just walked into the bar. I've been here for over an hour. You should be the one that leaves."

"Turn it off or leave!" he shouted again, his eyes wide with anger.

I was doing well to appear calm, but inside I was wobbling. A lot of people get bottled over the head in Pattaya, and I didn't want to be one of them.

"I'll finish my beer and leave," I said.

His friend walked over and said, "Fuck off now before there's trouble."

I figured it wasn't worth the hassle. I took one last drink of my beer and left. The previous night a German guy got pissed off with me for live streaming in a bar, and the previous week a couple of English guys tried to grab my phone when they saw me filming on Walking Street. I know some people don't like it, but it is not illegal to film in a public place. A lot of Youtubers live stream and make videos in downtown Pattaya, so if you really don't want to be caught on camera, then maybe Pattaya is not the place for you anymore.

After the argument with the two American lads, I couldn't bring myself to go into another bar and risk another confrontation, so I got a six pack of Leo beer and headed for the beach. I passed the freelancers standing under the palm trees along the promenade. I cracked open one of the beers and sat down on the cool night sand. I drank three beers in quick succession while I talked to my viewers, answering their questions and responding to their comments. A lot of my viewers were saying how jealous they were that I was living in Pattaya and how happy I must be to be living in the land of smiles, but I was feeling really down that night. Confrontations with fellow falangs were becoming ever more frequent, and it really bothered me.

After my third beer, I stood up and I suddenly felt quite drunk. I decided to walk it off. I was walking along the beach with my fourth beer in hand when I saw two Thai women up ahead, sitting on a couple of plastic stools in the sand. I noticed there were a couple of empty stools, so I asked if I could join them.

"Yes, yes," one of them said shyly.

As soon as I sat down, I explained that I was live streaming on Youtube. They didn't seem to understand what I was saying. Their English was poor, but we managed to start a very basic conversation. They told me their names and that they were from Bangkok. When I asked them their age at first, they answered in Thai and I couldn't understand. They tried to tell me their age in English too, but their pronunciation was terrible. I couldn't make out what they were saying.

"Do you want a beer?" I asked.

"No, no," they both replied when I tried to hand them a can.

"Go on. Have one beer."

"No, no, cannot," the one closest to me said, pushing the can away.

They started laughing and talking in Thai amongst themselves. I felt a little left out and unwelcome so I looked at the comments section in my live stream. Several of my viewers were writing the same comment over and over again, 'They said they are *sip hok* (16).'

I felt wobbly inside. I turned to the two girls and asked,

"You are sip hok?"

"Yes," they both replied in chorus.

I was surprised that they were so young. I often found it very hard to guess Thai girls' ages, but these girls were on the beach in Pattaya after midnight, so of course I assumed that they were adults. The thought never even occurred to me that they might be sixteen. Anyway, I grabbed my beer and split. The legal drinking age in Thailand is twenty, and there I was offering two sixteen year old girls beer on a beach late at night. It looked dodgy, and, worst of all, I had broadcasted the whole thing live on Youtube. When I got back to the promenade, I finished the live stream prematurely and headed straight back to my room. The night was a disaster. I deleted that live stream and tried to forget all about it.

After the beach incident, I took a break from live streaming for a few days. I needed to reassess my plans for my channel. Live streaming while I walked around Pattaya and hopped from bar to bar was a recipe for disaster. It was inevitable that I would end up getting in more arguments with falangs, Mamasans and perhaps bar girls too, and god help me if I happened to film a ladyboy who didn't want to be filmed. I also had to consider that I was drinking a lot on every live stream, so the more I walked around the streets and the more bars I drank in, the more likely I was to do something stupid and get in trouble. After several days of deep consideration, I decided to continue live streaming, but unlike before I would only live stream from two bars – Whoopers and Nikki's Bar, which was on a small soi off of Soi Buakhao. I chose Nikki's Bar because there were several girls and ladyboys in the bar, and whenever I went there, they all welcomed me warmly and seemed happy to be on camera.

People seemed to love my new live streams. I consistently got over four hundred viewers at a time, which was more than any other live streamer in Pattaya. I was also getting a lot of new subscribers. After a month of live streaming in Nikki's bar, I had about seven thousand subscribers. I had the same routine every night - two quick free beers in Whoopers and then I went to Nikki's Bar for the rest of the night, and on my way back to my room I stopped somewhere for a bowl of noodles or a plate of fried rice. During the hour in Whoopers, Craig turned the music down low so that my viewers could hear me clearly. I used that time to have a casual chat with my viewers and to answer any questions they might have for me. But in Nikki's Bar my live streams took on a life of their own. The girls and ladyboys would often push me out of the way and talk into the camera; they loved interacting with the viewers. Sometimes they even picked up the phone and walked around the bar filming the other girls. I let all this happen because it was a lot of fun and it was easy for me. I really lucked out with Nikki's Bar. There were three or four really pretty girls, and there were two attractive ladyboys too, so there was something for everybody in my live streams.

The live streaming was great for Nikki's Bar. The bar and bar girls became kind of famous in the Pattaya Youtube scene. The place became packed every night, and other Youtubers started to come to live stream too. The girls loved it because they were now working in one of the busiest bars in Pattaya, so they were making more money on lady drinks and barfines. Also, the viewers started sending Super Chats for me to buy their favorite girl or ladyboy a drink. The girls were raking it in from all directions, and I was getting a lot of Super Chats too. It was win-win for everyone, and best of all there were no crazy falangs trying to grab my camera or kick me out of the bar.

The girls knew that this was a great opportunity for them to make money, so they really played up to the camera - blowing kissing, caressing each other and even dancing on the pole in the middle of the bar in an attempt to excite viewers into sending money. Some of the girls in Nikki's Bar even set up their own Youtube channel. I couldn't excite the viewers like the girls could, but I certainly encouraged them to send money via Super Chats or to my Paypal account. I also set up a Patreon account, which allowed viewers to subscribe to my community for a monthly fee. Patreon members got access to some of my old deleted live streams and a couple of random videos here and there that were not made public on Youtube. Patreon was very handy. I had twenty-five members paying five dollars. That might not sound like much, but it was like free money every month.

Everyone was happy except for Craig. He started following my Youtube channel very closely, and he saw how popular Nikki's bar had become thanks to me. He started pestering me to promote his bar more.

"You only show my bar for one hour at the start of the night when it is quiet," he complained. "It looks boring. Of course nobody wants to come here."

Whoopers was just a normal bar with a couple of bar staff but no working girls, so I told Craig that if I live streamed from his bar all night I wouldn't get any Super Chats. I sensed that Whoopers was struggling to make a profit. Streaming in his bar for an hour every night was my way of helping Craig, but he wanted more. After a couple of weeks of constant bickering, we finally came to a deal whereby I would get fifty percent off my rent, and in return I would do a four-hour live stream from his bar once a week. We also had some T-shirts made with my Youtube channel's logo and his bar name printed on them, and I wore the T-shirt on a lot of my live streams. Craig was happy with all this, and his bar did start to get some more customers, but nothing like Nikki's Bar.

By now I had loads of different revenue streams: Youtube ads, Patreon, Super Chats and donations to my Paypal account. I was making about fifteen hundred US dollars a month. I could see a bright future for myself in Pattaya. I was still on a tourist visa and I did a quick visa run to Cambodia every month. It was a huge hassle, but it was also very risky because loads of people told me I would eventually be refused entry back into Thailand if I continued doing these visa runs. Thailand don't want falangs leaving and coming back on a new tourist visa every month. I decided to join a Thai language school and get an education visa. It was valid for ninety days but I could get it extended easily at the local immigration office. The language school was a big expense but it was worth it for the visa, and I was also genuinely interested in learning Thai. My classes were from 2 PM to 5 PM from Monday to Friday, and I had perfect attendance for the first couple of weeks. After that I started to go every other day. The school didn't seem to mind.

Nit was twenty-four years old (four years younger than me), she was average height for a Thai woman, slim and busty. Nit came into my life around the time I hit the ten-thousand subscribers mark. She was working in a girly bar on Walking Street, but she often came to Nikki's Bar late at night to hang out with her friend, Nok, who was one of the bar girls. One night, Nok and Nit asked me to go to a club with them after the bar closed. One thing led to another and I ended up spending the night with Nit. Even for a bar girl, Nit's English was poor, but it was amazing how we just clicked and felt comfortable in each other's company from the start. We hung out together all day, and then she had to head off to work in her bar. Every night for about three weeks Nit and I hooked up after my live stream and spent the night together. Eventually we agreed that she should quit her job and move in with me. I told her I would pay for all her daily expenses, like food and drink, and that I would try to give her extra money for herself every week, but I couldn't commit to an exact figure. The thing I loved about Nit was that she was really laid back for a bar girl. She never pushed me for money and she was not moody or fake like most bar girls. She was a really genuine, kind and fun-loving girl.

As soon as Nit moved in with me, she became a big part of my live streams. To be honest, it was awkward bringing her to Nikki's Bar as my official girlfriend at first because during the previous few months I had made my way through everyone in the bar, including Nok, the Mamasan and even the two ladyboys. Nit must have heard all about it from Nok, but she never mentioned it to me. She never suggested that we stop going to Nikki's bar, and she never got jealous when I talked to any of the girls. As I said, she was a really cool, laid back girl. She was a gem. As well as being a great girlfriend, Nit also proved to be a very good live streaming partner. I had become sick of going out and getting pissed every night, but I kept it up for longer than I should have because I was worried that if I took a break even for a day or two, my channel might lose momentum. But now that I had Nit by my side, I could live stream from my room a couple of nights a week, or go out to dinner with Nit and talk to my viewers over a nice Thai meal in a quiet setting. Most viewers seemed to enjoy having a Thai woman in the live streams because she was eye candy. However, there were a few people who took an instant dislike to Nit, and they wrote some horrible things about her in the comments section. Apart from her large breasts, the most striking thing about Nit's appearance were her braces. I thought they made her look cute, but the trolls ridiculed her, calling her 'metal mouth', 'the crusher' and all sorts. My channel had a lot of trolls and they took great joy in dishing out abuse. Fortunately, Nit didn't understand most of the comments.

I seemed to have more trolls than other Pattaya Youtubers. They flocked to my channel because I didn't have any moderators during my live streams. Usually live streamers assign friends or trusted subscribers as moderators. Their job is to moderate the comments section by deleting anything inappropriate and banning repeat offenders. This was a good way to keep the comments section clean, but I didn't want to use moderators because I didn't want to sensor my viewers. The problem with this liberal approach was that it attracted trolls and allowed them to say the nastiest shit they could think of. The more popular my channel became, the more trolls I got. I had to develop thick skin quickly. 'Fat fuck!', 'Chain smoking dirty falang', 'Pervy sex tourist', 'Too fat and ugly to find a girl in your own country', 'Exploiting Thai women is disgraceful' – these are just some of the comments I got on a daily basis. In a weird way, the trolls became a big part of my channel because they gave me something to talk about during the live streams, and the comments section became very heated whenever the trolls and my subscribers argued with each other. But then things got out of hand.

Shortly after Nit moved in with me, my life as a Pattaya Youtuber started to get a bit fucked up, not because of Nit but because of a group who called themselves the 'GOP' (Guards of Pattaya). I had learned to live with the trolls, but these fuckers stepped way over the line. The GOP was the name of a Youtube channel. They claimed to be a group, but really they could have just been one sad spotty, specky teenager living with his mom back in England. The purpose of the GOP's Youtube channel was to attack Pattaya Youtubers. They claimed that we were filming people against their will, taking advantage of Thai women and disrespecting Thai culture. It didn't start off too bad. First, they started putting up clips of my live streams. They took some thirty second clips of me saying something disrespectful about bar girls, and then they put half a dozen of these clips together to make a short video. Then they uploaded a video of me pleading strongly with viewers to send money for beer, and they called me an 'E-beggar' – someone who begs online. Sometimes when I got drunk, I did go a bit too far by pleading desperately with my viewers to send Super Chats. I admit it. And, look, to be honest, I'm not a good drunk sometimes, so when I've had a few too many to drink, I tend to say and do some really stupid stuff. Sometimes when I woke up in the morning with a hungover, I deleted the live stream from the night before because I was so embarrassed about something I had said or done. But the reason the GOP were such a pain in the ass was because they were able to upload clips from my old live streams that I had deleted as soon as the live stream had stopped. This means that they must have somehow been recording my live streams on their computer. They caught all my worst moments, like when I went on a ten-minute rant about other

Pattaya Youtubers, saying how they were all perverts. And they even got a clip of me admitting to my viewers that I had been with the two ladyboys in Nikki's Bar. On average I filmed for about four hours almost every night, so the GOP had plenty of material to work with. They always found some angle, some new rod to whip me with. The videos always got about a thousand views because the GOP and other trolls mentioned the videos on my live streams and probably on other Youtube channels too.

When the GOP first started making videos on Youtube, they attacked half a dozen different Youtubers in Pattaya. I won't mention any names, but one of the Youtubers they went after was an American guy who used to go crazy when he drank too much. He would scream into the camera and start threatening his trolls and other Youtubers with violence. Those clips were gold for the GOP. There was also a French guy who desperately pleaded for money every night on his live streams. They called him the 'King of E-beggars'. But after a while, the GOP really started focusing on me, perhaps because my channel was growing quickly. Things started to get really bad after Nit said my full name during one of the live streams by mistake. The GOP obviously took note of my name and searched the internet for information on me, because the next day they uploaded a short video with embarrassing old pictures from my old Myspace page. I was only nineteen in the photos. I was sitting in my living room with spiky hair and a shiny light blue shirt. It was cringe. A few days later they stepped things up a notch and made a video with a couple of pictures of my sister. My sister! They were dragging my family into this. I was furious. Fortunately, my sister never saw the video. I never told my family that I had a Youtube channel because I didn't want them to see me getting drunk and hanging out with bar girls every night.

After they showed pictures of my sister, I thought the GOP couldn't go any lower, but the following week they put up a video of me asking my viewers to send Nit money to help her pay her dentist fees, and at the end of the video they showed a scanned copy of the main page in my passport. Everything was clearly visible – my picture, my full name (including my middle name), and my passport number. *This can't be legal*, I thought. I reported the video to Youtube, and I got some of my most loyal subscribers to report it too. A few days later, Youtube removed the video and the GOP's channel, but it didn't do much good because every time I reported them, they just set up another channel with a slightly different name and uploaded their backlog of videos again, including the video with my passport.

The passport stunt was an incredible breach of my privacy. I couldn't figure out how they had gotten a hold of a scanned copy of my passport in the first place. One night, when I was on my way back to my room after Nikki's Bar, I ran into Craig downstairs and I accused him of giving the GOP a scanned copy of my passport.

"You're the only one in Pattaya who has a copy of my passport," I blurted out.

"Dickhead," he started, outraged by the accusation, "when you arrived here, you wrote your passport details in our check-in form, but you never handed over your passport, so how could I scan it?"

Craig was right. I never even showed him my passport. I apologized sincerely and went up to bed. The only people who had a scanned copy of my passport were the staff in my Thai language school. I never mentioned the name of my school on any of my live streams, but there couldn't be more than a dozen schools for falangs in Pattaya. The GOP knew my name, so it would have been easy enough for them to call all the schools and inquire about me. How they got the staff to talk, and how they managed to get the staff to hand over the scanned copy, I don't know, but we all know that money talks in Thailand. A couple of thousand baht to the right person would have done the job, I reckon. I considered confronting the head of the school about this issue, but I decided to let it drop because I was worried that he would get angry and kick me out of the course. If that happened, my education visa would be cancelled.

For a while it looked like the GOP was running out of material to attack me with. They kept uploading old clips of me acting a bit daft during my live streams, but it was nothing major. Perhaps because they had no other rocks to throw at me, the GOP started a campaign on Youtube to have me deported from Thailand on the basis that I was on an education visa but I was earning money through Youtube advertizing and Super Chats. They made a new video every day with clips of me getting Super Chats from viewers. At the end of each video they showed my passport page and the number of Thai immigration. They implored people to report me. As far as I know, Thai law is not very clear on this issue. I had never heard of anyone being deported from Thailand because they were earning money on Youtube, so I wasn't really worried. Their campaign looked kind of weak and desperate to me, but then they uploaded a clip of me offering beer to the two sixteen-year-old girls on the beach. This time they urged people to report me to immigration on the grounds that I had broken the law and that I was a threat to society. The clip got over twenty thousand views within a week. They got someone to translate the clip into Thai and they spread it all over social media so that Thai people could see what I had done. When my viewers asked me about this issue on my live stream, I just played the whole thing down and laughed it off, but inside I was worried. It suddenly seemed possible that the police might get involved. The GOP even made a video to announce that the police were looking for me, but that was bullshit! As I said at the time, I went to the same two bars almost every night, and I went to a Thai language school at the same time every other day, so if the police really were looking for me, I wouldn't be very hard to find. A few days later, the GOP contradicted themselves by saying that in order for the police to take action, they needed a full, unedited version of the live stream in which I offered the girls beer. The GOP obviously didn't have the full live stream, so they reached out to viewers for help. I still don't know if the police really did request a full, unedited version of the live stream, but after a few weeks it all blew over and the GOP moved on to accusing me of taking and selling drugs.

The accusations of me being a drug user and a drug dealer were groundless. They literally had no evidence to support their accusations. They showed one video clip of me taking something out of my wallet discreetly and slipping it to an Australian guy I was drinking with in Nikki's Bar, and the GOP took that as proof that I was dealing. But it was ridiculous; I was actually giving the guy a condom. He was about to go back to his hotel with one of the bar girls, and he didn't want to stop in a 7eleven on the way to buy condoms, so I gave him one. I wanted to save his blushes, so I slipped it to him discreetly. That's all there was to it. I really thought this campaign to portray me as a drug dealer would be over after a couple of days, but the GOP kept at it for weeks, posting the same video over and over again. It was crazy. Fortunately, those videos got hardly any views. People must have seen how stupid the accusations were. It looked like the whole thing was fizzling out, but one day after my Thai class, the Director of the school – a Thai man in his late fifties, always in a nice suit - called me into his office and told me that I could no longer attend classes. I was shocked.

"Why?" I asked.

"We get emails and telephone calls about you," he explained. "Maybe ten emails and twenty calls every day only about you."

"What about?" I was confused.

"Some say you do drug. Some say you sell drug. Some say different things about young girls and making trouble and showing bad things on the internet."

"But it's not true," I said strongly. "This isn't fair. I shouldn't be banned from the school just because a few people called and told lies about me."

"I don't know if they are lies or not, but it not good for our school. It is important we have a good reputation. If you come our school, it will not be good for our school's name."

I fell back in my seat and sighed deeply. This was a disaster.

"What will happen with my education visa?"

"We will tell immigration you not come here anymore and your visa will be cancelled."

I sat in silence for a few minutes. It was a lot to take in. To his credit, the Director was nice about it all. He didn't judge me or try to rush me out the door.

"What about my money?" I asked.

The Director checked my payment status on his computer and said, "You already pay for one year, so we can refund you the remaining months."

I had an idea.

"How about this?" I said, excited inside. "I will not come to classes anymore but please do not report it to immigration. If you agree, you don't need to give me a refund. You can keep the money and I can keep my visa."

The Director turned to his computer screen again as he considered my proposition. Perhaps he was calculating the size of the possible refund. He closed his eyes to think some more. Eventually he looked at me with a solemn face and said, "Okay. I no tell immigration. I no make problem for your visa."

I walked out of the office that day feeling good because I had saved my precious visa, but when I had time to reflect on what had happened, I started to feel really down about the situation. The GOP had screwed me over. They were relentless and they were now affecting my life in a very real way. I needed to get away from Pattaya for a while. Nit and I packed our stuff and we headed off to Ko Samet for a few days.

Nit saw how stressed I was because of the GOP, so she made a rule 'No Youtube' in Ko Samet. Bless Nit. She always supported me no matter what shit I was going through. Some viewers slated her for only being with me for money, and the trolls hated on me for paying to be with Nit, but our relationship wasn't just about money. It was legit. We cared about each other and always treated each other with respect. To be honest, we never argued about money because we had a clear and simple arrangement: I used the money from Youtube to pay for accommodation, food, drink and travel expenses, and I gave her two thousand baht spending money every week. She rarely spent any of the two thousand baht and I never asked her about it, so I guess she put it in her bank account and sent it back home. It wasn't a lot of money but she seemed satisfied with it.

While we were on Ko Samet, I broke the 'No Youtube' rule

almost every waking hour of every day. Of course I checked the views on my videos and the money I was getting from advertisements, but I also constantly checked the GOP's videos. By this time they had multiple channels in case one of them got taken down by Youtube. In one of their videos, they had screenshots showing their email correspondence with the Director of my Thai language school. The last email was of the Director explaining that he had removed me from the school because of multiple complaints. Not that I needed it, but this was proof that the GOP were behind all the phone calls and emails to the school. They seemed so proud of their little victory.

It was on Ko Samet that I first heard about the Corona virus. I didn't think much of it at first. I just heard there was a new flu-like virus in China, but at that time the majority of the cases were in one city. I was back in Pattaya a few weeks when things started getting serious and I could see the effects of Corona first hand. Certain parts of Pattaya, like Walking Street and Beach Road, were often packed with huge groups of tourists during the day, but overnight the Chinese tourists stopped coming because they were in lockdown back in their own country. It didn't really feel like a big deal at first because the Chinese tourists usually don't go to the girly bars anyway, so Pattaya's nightlife seemed to go on as normal. It was only during the daytime that you would notice that certain places were much quieter than normal. The virus started spreading in small numbers to dozens of countries around the world. Due to the close proximity of Thailand to China, and of course the huge amounts of Chinese tourists who visit Thailand, Thai people and the government were understandably worried that there would be a huge outbreak of Corona in the kingdom. Initially, a one-month state of emergency was announced. There was a curfew that banned all people from leaving their homes from 10 PM to 4 AM. All travel into Thailand stopped, and soon all bars and other entertainment venues were forced to close. Restaurants could still remain open, but only for take-out. If you were caught violating any of these rules, you could be sent to jail for up to two and a half years and/or be fined forty thousand baht. As you can imagine, Pattaya was devastated by these measures. No more tourists for the hotels, bars, restaurants, markets, taxis or stores, and nowhere for the thousands of bar girls to work. Most of the workers in the service industry left Pattaya and went back to stay with their families in the countryside while they waited for the pandemic to blow over. But not everybody left Pattaya. Some people had no family so they had no choice but to stay. A lot of the people that were left behind were poor and hungry, so volunteer groups set up free food stalls. One of these stalls was set up on Sao Buakhao. I could see it from my window. The queue was often a hundred people long. It was sad to see.

Pattaya is my second home. During Thai national holidays the selling of alcohol is strictly forbidden, but I know a place that will sell me as much beer as I want, no matter how sacred the holiday. Convenience stores in Thailand can only sell alcohol during certain hours of the day, but I know a mama and papa store that will sell me beer twenty-four hours a day. In Pattaya there's always a way. Even when the Thai government introduced a curfew and shut down all the bars, I wasn't worried because I knew that some bars would secretly open. Nit and I live streamed from our room for a while, but then a mate of mine told me about a bar that was accepting customers.

I can't say the name or the exact location of the bar, but let's just say it was within a stone's throw of Soi Buakhao. I was well known in the bar, both by the owner and the staff, so I knew I'd be welcomed. Nit and I ate instant noodles in our room for dinner and headed out shortly before 10 PM. Pattaya is usually bright even at night because of the countless Neon lights on almost every street. That's probably why the government never bothered putting up many street lights. But during the lockdown the streets of Pattaya were dark and empty. Of course all the bars and a lot of the restaurants were closed, but even some of the 7elevens were closed. I had never seen that before in Thailand. They are always open – twenty-four hours a day, every day – but not during Corona. When we arrived at the bar, the shutters were down and all the lights were off. Two women were walking behind us, so we waited for them to pass and walk out of sight. I put my ear up to the shutters and listened carefully. I couldn't hear anything. *My mate lied to me,* I thought. *There's no way this place is open.* I was ready to walk away, but Nit knocked on the iron shutters gently and said something in Thai. No answer. She tried again. This time we heard footsteps coming towards us. Then a male voice whispered something in Thai. Nit answered back. We heard the jangling of keys and the sound of a padlock being opened. I looked up and down the street quickly to make sure the coast was clear. When I looked back, the shutters were being pulled up quickly and I could see that the Thai man on the other side was Tee, the owner of the bar. There was no time for greetings. He signaled for us to get inside quickly before someone saw us.

The bar was completely dark and all the seats were empty. When Tee locked the shutters again, he turned his phone torch on and used it to lead us to the back. Towards the back of the bar there was a small separate area with two tables. There was no door, but Tee put up a black curtain to block the light. When we walked through the door curtain, I was glad to see some familiar faces and some pretty Thai women. There were six people (four falang guys and two Thai women) sitting at the two tables, drinking beer and looking like they were having a good time. I knew all four of the guys but neither of the girls. Nobody minded being on camera, so I set up my phone and started live streaming straight away. A lot of my viewers were delighted to see me out and about again, but some of the haters started complaining in the comments section about how I was breaking Thai law by drinking in a bar during lockdown. The GOP even joined the live stream and urged people to copy the video and send it to Thai immigration. I wasn't too worried. Other haters said it was careless and selfish of me to be out socializing during the lockdown, and that by doing so I was putting myself and others at risk. But the number of cases in Thailand were very low. There were only about ten new cases a day in the whole country, and, as far as I knew, none of the new cases were in Pattaya. Also, I was helping out a local business. If it wasn't for me and the four other falangs secretly drinking in the bar, Tee wouldn't have had any money coming in during the lockdown. I explained all this on the live stream, but the haters were a stubborn bunch. They were never willing to see the good in what I was doing.

A couple of hours into the live stream, Tee sat with us for a beer and talked with me on camera. He was only on camera for about two minutes, but during that short time he let slip the name of his bar. I turned the camera away from him quickly and didn't let him speak on the live stream again. I really hoped that nobody had picked up on the name of the bar, but within thirty seconds of him saying it, people were typing it over and over again in the comments section. And the GOP left a comment saying that they had just reported me and the bar to the police. I told everyone in the bar what was happening. Nobody took the GOP's threat seriously except for Nit. She wanted to leave immediately because she remembered the incident at the Thai language school and she knew what the GOP were capable of. I knew that the safest option was to leave and run back to our room, but I was a little drunk by now and wild horses couldn't have dragged me away from the party.

Soon we heard a car pull up outside the bar. Tee turned off the light and whispered, "Turn off phones everyone."

The doors of the car opened and closed. All was silent for a few minutes, and then someone started banging on the shutters.

"Everyone hide in toilets," Tee whispered.

All eight of us hurried to the toilets on tiptoes. It didn't matter about gender. I ended up in the women's toilet with Nit, one of the Thai girls and one of the falangs. The toilets were tiny. We were cramped together like sardines and Nit had to stand on the toilet seat. We were all a little drunk, but we realized the seriousness of the situation. I didn't actually think I would be sent to prison if I was caught, but I knew I would be in big trouble with immigration, and of course there would be a forty thousand baht fine to pay. We waited anxiously in the toilet. There was no fan or air conditioning, and it was a tight space with four people pressed up against each other and breathing heavily. The sweat was pouring off of us. I kept the live stream going, but I pointed the camera to the ground and didn't talk.

We were there for about ten minutes before Tee came and said, "Okay. Come out. Police go already."

I was instantly giddy with relief. The party resumed and we continued drinking until the early hours of the morning. It gave me great pleasure to think how pissed off the GOP must have been that I wasn't caught.

Nit and I never went back to that bar again because it was too risky. Over the next few weeks we had a couple of nights out in other bars that were secretly accepting customers, but it wasn't really worth it because for some reason viewers were not sending Super Chats during this period. It felt like I was wasting my time, so I started live streaming only twice a week, and those live streams were of just me and Nit drinking in our room and responding to the comments section. In an attempt to get more

Super Chats, I announced that I would do some challenges during the live streams. First, I set myself the challenge of eating seven Big Macs in thirty minutes. A few days later I announced that I would try to drink ten beers in an hour. I completed both challenges successfully and I got about five thousand baht in Super Chats for each challenge. But apart from those two occasions, the Super Chats were few and far between for well over a month. I had to dip into my savings for a while. Fortunately, I had saved quite a bit before Corona hit.

Eventually Pattaya started to open up a little. Nit and I started going out again as soon as the bars opened, but it wasn't much fun. There were hardly any customers and the bars had to close early. My live streams suffered as a result. At the end of one of our nights out, Nit invited three of her friends back to our room for a party. Great idea! We got food and a load of beers from 7eleven and continued our live stream back in our room. The viewers loved it. They were sending money to get the girls to dance and drink more. The Super Chats reached the levels of the golden days in Nikki's Bar. At the end of the live stream I gave each of the girls five hundred baht, and I made them promise to come back the next night. The girls couldn't believe their luck. They got five hundred baht for drinking beer with their friends and dancing a bit, not to mention the free food and drink. The next night we met up with the three girls again and live streamed from a private room in a karaoke bar. This time I trained the girls a little. Before the live stream started, I told them to act shy and reserved at first. Then I told the viewers that the girls only start dancing when they are a little drunk. When I said that, the Super Chats started pouring in. Each Super Chat came with a message, 'Drink for the girls', 'Drink up' and so on. It worked a treat. Easy money.

I stumbled upon a new formula for my live streams: bring a bunch of girls to a private room and live stream with them drinking and dancing. Sometimes we live stream from our room, sometimes from a karaoke bar, and sometimes we travel to nearby cities for a change of scenery. We also change the girls every few days. Nit knows a lot of girls around Pattaya, so finding new blood is never a problem. I can even pick and choose the perfect mix of women for every live stream. I always ask Nit to find a skinny, pretty one in her early twenties, a busty one and a ladyboy. I figure that is the perfect mix because there is something there for all tastes. It isn't always possible to get all those types in one live stream, but we try to get some kind of variety at least.

The GOP are still disgusted by my live streams. They say that I am pimping the girls out and taking advantage of them. But the girls would be the first to say that is bullshit! These days if I get a good amount of Super Chats during the live stream, I give the girls anywhere from one thousand to two thousand baht each. That's good money for them, especially during Corona. There are precious few customers in Pattaya, so if it wasn't for my live streams the girls would have no way of making money. The GOP still make videos about me almost every day. They still show my passport details, and they call me an E-beggar, a pimp, a fat bastard, and the most hated Youtuber in Pattaya, but I still get new subscribers every day and the Super Chats keep coming. My record amount of Super Chats for one night is two thousand dollars. There's no stopping me now.